Business Ethics in the Global Market

T0167631

Edited by Tibor R. Machan

Business Ethics in the Global Market

Hoover Institution Press Stanford University Stanford, California *www.hoover.org*

Hoover Institution Press Publication No. 455
Hoover Institution at Leland Stanford Junior University,
Stanford, California 94305

First printing, 1999
23 22 21 20 19 18 17 16 15   13 12 11 10 9 8 7 6 5

Manufactured in the United States of America
The paper used in this publication meets the minimum requirements of American National Standard for Information Sciences—Permanence of Paper for Printed Library Materials, ANSI Z39.48–1992. ♾

Library of Congress Cataloging-in-Publication Data
Business ethics in the global market / edited by Tibor R. Machan.
        p.   cm. — (Hoover Institution Press publication ; no. 455)
Includes bibliographical references and index.
ISBN 978-0-8179-9632-1 (pbk : alk. paper)
ISBN 978-0-8179-9633-8 (epub)
ISBN 978-0-8179-9637-6 (mobi)
ISBN 978-0-8179-9638-3 (PDF)
1. Business ethics.   2. International trade—Moral and ethical aspects.
I. Machan, Tibor R.   II. Series: Hoover Institution Press Publication ; 455.
HF5387.B87238   1999
174'.4—dc21   99-25882
                                                              CIP

Contents

Contributors

TIBOR R. MACHAN is professor at the Argyros School of Business and Economics, Chapman University, and research fellow at the Hoover Institution, Stanford University.

ROBERT W. MCGEE is a professor at the W. Paul Stillman School of Business, Seton Hall University.

ELLEN FRANKEL PAUL is professor of political science and philosophy, Bowling Green State University, and deputy director of the Social Philosophy and Policy Center.

AMARTYA K. SEN is master of Trinity College, Cambridge University, and recipient of the 1998 Nobel Prize in economic sciences.

DR. ELAINE STERNBERG is a fellow in Philosophy at the University of Leeds, and principal of Analytical Solutions, a London consultancy firm specializing in business ethics and corporate governance.

Tibor R. Machan

Introduction:
Norms of Business Abroad

Business ethics is a division of professional ethics, itself a branch of what is sometimes called role ethics—which includes such fields as parental, political, fraternal, and other special areas concerned with how a sound ethical theory is to be applied to the various distinct areas of human life.

Ethics is a controversial branch of philosophy, addressing the questions "How should one act?" or "What standards of conduct guide a good human life?" It is controversial for several reasons, among them the perennial problem of whether human beings are free agents, capable of initiating or causing their own action. If the answer is that they are not, that everything we do is the result of factors that determine what we do and we are simply being moved to behave as we must given these causal factors, then ethics is impossible or must be understood as proclivities or tendencies a healthy person follows but others have somehow been prevented from following. Praise or blame for what we do, then, is misguided—at most they are prompters or encouragements to behave as would be preferable. But no credit or liability could be attached to what we do since, in the last analysis, we as individual agents are not responsible for what we do.

There is also the highly controversial issue of whether ethics is a cognitive field, one wherein knowledge may be gained and used. Many contend that it is not and that, instead, ethical claims are disguised emotional preferences, positive or negative attitudes, and so on. Since the time of David Hume it has been widely believed—leaving a serious legacy on how many people see the nature of ethics and other studies of human affairs—that facts are separated by an unbridgeable gap from values, the "is" from the "ought." This has tended to remove ethics from the domain of rational discussion, science, and such and to place it within realms of faith such as religion and theology.

Even if ethics is a bona fide concern, even if we can act on our own initiative, and even if facts are relevant to how we ought to act, ethics remains controversial in virtue of the extensive dispute about just what it is, most generally, that we ought to do, what standards are right for us to follow, and whether any one approach will do the task of guiding human conduct as such. Ethical theories attempt to address that issue, each aiming to answer the question "How should we act?" correctly, truly. Such theories as hedonism, utilitarianism, altruism, egoism, and a host of other less familiar ones have competed for that right answer to the question of ethics. More generally, there is argument about whether human values are structured systematically or are more disorderly, even contradictory.

This would suggest that there is little advance one can make in the effort to address the field of applied ethics. Which theory should guide us for purposes of applying ethics to such special areas? Although various moral philosophers have argued to their own satisfaction for the soundness of one or another ethical theory, no consensus is at hand. And this should not be surprising—the problem of ethics is so basic to human living that every generation of philosophers will probably have to reexamine the issue anew, with only so much help gained from earlier efforts. Human beings tend not to accept what their elders have identified, argued, even established to their own intellectual and practical satisfaction. This itself suggests strongly that human beings are not hardwired to do the right thing but need to figure it out or learn it from those who have done so.

Still, some points can be drawn on from the history of moral philosophy that can at least help us to make progress with the issues involved. For one, just as in other fields of knowledge, in the field of ethics we have certain commonsense beliefs that have developed and can provide us with certain initial clues. Those commonsense ethical precepts are the ones most people have in mind when they use such terms as *ethical, moral, acceptable, appropriate* in characterizing human conduct. Although they will not be the same from one age to the next, from one culture to another, from one religion to others, there are some core principles we tend to find embraced everywhere, taught to children, demanded of professionals, used to criticize politicians, public figures, and neighbors or professional associates.

For purposes of understanding business ethics the most crucial issue to be addressed is whether business is itself a profession that can be practiced ethically, morally. Without first addressing fully which ethical theory is sound, we can at least consider whether by reference to commonsense ethics the field of business—or, more generally, commerce—has moral standing.

For a profession to have moral standing, it needs to accord with some of the virtues that ought to guide our lives. Medicine, law, education, science, and so on are all professions that fulfill some good—health, justice, rearing children, knowledge, and so on. Is there any virtue that commerce fulfills as ordinarily conducted? That is to say, as people engage in trade and its various elements—producing goods and services for sale, advertising, purchasing goods and services, managing firms, marketing, and so on—are they doing something that is morally commendable or, at least, unobjectionable?

Based on simple commonsense ethics, business activities qualify as an exercise of the moral virtue of prudence. This virtue requires of us all to take reasonably good care of ourselves in life, give support to the effort to prosper, to seek to profit. Business specializes in producing prosperity. It has moral standing because it is what may be called the institutionalization of the virtue of prudence. And although this alone does not indicate how important a moral virtue guides business—whether prudence is a major or minor virtue, very important for us all or only applicable in certain circumstances—it does support the view that, contrary to what some argue (namely, that "business ethics" is an oxymoron), there is virtue in doing business, in engaging in commerce.

In this volume we consider an even narrower topic than business ethics as such. We are going to consider what business ethics has to say about trade conducted with people outside one's own society, on the global market. Our authors examine different areas of this issue. But in the back of their analysis lies the basic idea that there is nothing inherently morally objectionable about business as such. It is not true what Charles Baudelaire said, namely, that "commerce is satanic, because it is the basest and vilest form of egoism."

Yet because business is morally OK, just as is science, education, art, or athletics, it still faces ethical challenges. At the day-to-day level of business practices we find that questions arise about what should guide decisions about hiring, firing, promotion, reprimanding someone, advertising to certain potential customers, and so forth. Need one tell the whole truth in advertising, or is it more appropriate to think of such a task as promotion, where just part of the truth will suffice, provided it is the truth? People in business also need to figure out how to balance their various responsibilities—family, friendship, citizenship, recreation, and so on—in ways that are morally sound. More broadly, what are the principles of bona fide competition? Is it proper for a firm to call on the Department of Justice to try to contend with another's superior performance? Are closed-shop practices morally acceptable? Should one lobby for subsidies or price supports, let alone monopoly privileges granted by governments? What about promoting tariffs or duties against foreign competitors? How about the issue of moving a company abroad where regulations, but also criminal laws, might pose less hindrance to economic success? It is here that we are beginning to touch on issues that will be dealt with in this work.

The main problem about doing business abroad—which is to say, embarking on commerce with people and organizations apart from one's familiar Western environment—is that the monetary terms are favorable and may seriously tempt business agents to breach certain moral principles in order to take advantage of them. From major corporations to nearly all consumers purchasing low-cost products made by workers in, say, China, Indonesia, Malaysia, Korea, or Mexico, the terms are sweet. But this sometimes comes at the expense of becoming wicked. Some of these countries are, as the Soviet Union or South Africa used to be, greater or lesser tyrannies ruled by some more or less oppressive elites. To cooperate one can easily taint one's soul, sully one's character.

Contrary to some prominent views in our day (e.g., those of Richard Rorty) all this cannot be managed by way of what has come to be referred to as Asian (or Latin or some other) versus Western community values. The notion that freedom of trade, free markets, voluntary economic interaction, and so on, happens to be one type of practice (e.g., Western) among many equally valid systems of practices (so that no decisions can be made which suit human beings better) is troublesome. This impulse—call it relativism or solidarism—arises out of a typically modern concern. It is whether values—moral, political, what-

ever—can have an objective basis. Of course, such epistemologi-
cal worries ultimately infect not just values (ethical, political, and
aesthetic principles) but science and all claims to human knowledge. What is pertinent here is that the very idea of professional,
including business, ethics flies in the face of such cultural and
related relativism.

Our concerns about business ethics in the global market stem
not so much from whether ethics is possible at all but, rather,
from many Western consumers—and the producers who want
to earn a living from serving them—wishing to have it both
ways. Those addressing the topic either abstractly or in their
actual business dealings wish to stand up for the principles of
free citizenship and market agency while also, at least tempo-
rarily, hoping to benefit from economic opportunities that rest
on the violations of basic moral and political principles in those
countries where cost of production, labor, transportation, legal
compliance, and government regulation are all minimal.

Of course, no country is "morally and political pure," with a
citizenry and leadership that's completely decent and just. But a
country that legally tolerates, for example, slave labor on a wide
scale is certainly worse than one that has some draconian envi-
ronmental policies, if only because the latter at least has a chance
to be negotiated via the political process. That is pretty elemen-
tary—the difference between petty and draconian tyrannies, that
is, and the existence of a continuum between the least and the
most dictatorial in the realm of commerce within a culture.

Still, concern of how to relate to such countries cannot be
evaded by anyone who is concerned with leading a decent human life, including in the capacity of a professional merchant or
business executive. Countries can change, and even the worst of
them may have some valuable aspects that make contact with its
people, including on the commercial front, demonstrably worth-
while.

In short, we can ask quite meaningfully—and should do so on and off—"How should we approach doing business with the people of China, for example, given the country's nature as a great or lesser tyranny?" It is the task of the discipline of professional ethics—pertaining to medicine, law, education, science, art, or business—to examine the ethical challenges posed by distinct regions of productive human activity. In the field of business, this includes coming to terms with ethical challenges faced while doing business abroad, while interacting with members of different cultures, religions, political traditions, cultural practices. The question that is at issue is "What special ethical problems arise for people—for managers and employees of companies, firms—when they embark on their commercial tasks in countries and cultures other than their own?"

The essays in this work address various aspects of this question and propose various responses to it. But they are united by something rare in such discussions: a lack of distrust of free men and women engaged in commerce whose actions are circumscribed by public policies and laws that do not dictate to business agents any more than they do to journalists or the clergy. In short, this book discusses business ethics for a free market—specifically, on the global level. I only spell out some of the most basic principles that such a discussion will most likely presuppose, although individual authors may not consider this exactly the way to frame the point. No complete congruence can be expected of creative scholars, in any case, and simply because of some uniting convictions the authors in the book need not speak with one voice.

Laws are not uniform throughout the world, or even within one's own country. In the United States of America and some other nations throughout the globe a relatively free market tradition of business and trade prevails. This means that the laws, to a greater extent than elsewhere, tend to protect the right to private property and the integrity of terms of trade and contractual arrangements. This means that negative individual rights may not be violated with impunity. Government interference in the United States, for example, and to a greater extent in other Western countries, is substantial but exists as something of an anomaly, an exception to the general ethos or style of doing commercial work. In short, in contrast to other societies, a U.S. citizen lives in a near-capitalist economy, as do, to a lesser extent, the citizens of many other so-called Western countries.

The governments of most societies are not based on liberal principles of social living—namely, respect for and protection of individual rights to life, liberty and property. Rather, they are frequently the owners and operators of business enterprises and make it possible to carry out trade while the right to freedom for the citizens is seriously compromised (e.g., via the use of slave labor, heavy subsidization, and monopolization throughout various industries, a near-command economy that is loosening often only because the government—the legitimacy of which is in serious dispute from the framework of constitutional democracies or republics—sees that as useful for a given purpose).

Professionals doing business have as their special goal—qua professional businesspeople—to make their enterprise prosper, to earn a profit. They tend to focus on this goal as against others in their professional thinking and conduct. Of course, artists striving to express their visions do no less, or educators, scientists, or athletes. Normally, when no moral dilemmas arise from embarking on one's professional tasks, this is unobjectionable from the point of view of ethics. When scientists search for truth in their specialty, it is not morally objectionable that they neglect, say, justice or generosity while wearing their scientist hats, as it were. Educators, even as they talk at great length about social problems, do not at that time do anything much about them.

They are teaching others to think about them who may or may not put this to practical use.

However, people often become single-minded, acquire "tunnel vision," as they fulfill some special role in their lives. As parents, friends, or citizens we are often willing to overlook considerations bearing on our general, broad human—that is, moral—responsibilities in the course of pursuing our goals. The task of living a decent human life is often compromised by intently focusing on special objectives. In business, as in other professions, this can result in being willing to achieve goals—for example, to make money—from circumstances that involve serious moral improprieties, even out-and-out violations of the basic rights of human beings. When scientists use unwilling subjects for experimentation, educators metamorphose into indoctrinators or those in business become, even if only indirectly, thieves or masters over unwilling subjects—they still see themselves as pursuing their professional goals but are, in fact, doing so at great moral cost. And if one realizes that the greatest, most important goal is to excel as a human being, to remain on the moral up-and-up, this comes to no less that self-betrayal, in the last analysis.

Suppose some firm in China, run by the military arm of the government, uses coerced labor to produce various goods or services at very low cost. This is partly because the workers and managers are forced by their oppressive governments to take low pay, partly because the absence of organized labor makes collective bargaining impossible, partly because lack of free markets prevents wage competition that could lead to higher (or lower) pay.

The usual excuse, when ethical points are raised against doing business with such organizations, is that if a given firm refuses to do business for various moral reasons, others will take advantage of the opportunities at hand. Alternatively, we are told that it would betray stockholders to forgo doing business abroad when faced with clear economic opportunities. (Some invoke Milton Friedman's thesis about the sole moral responsibility of business being making a profit, yet even Friedman modifies this by saying that it needs to be done within the rules of the game, ethics, and just law!)

None of the excuses offered are relevant to whether one ought to conduct business ethically, anymore than they would excuse any other sort of conduct involving the violation of people's rights—as when a doctor who uses unwilling subjects intones about the greater good his results will reap for future generations. (If one uses unwilling members of current generations for the sake of those in the future, those in the future are certainly at serious risk rather than being benefited.) Stealing and other such violations of individual rights can often be economically or otherwise advantageous, at least in the short run. Muggers, plagiarizers, embezzlers, and bank robbers all pursue their goals of obtaining wealth or other kinds of advantage, but the means by which they do it are morally and thus decisively wrong. This is no less so when people in business pursue policies that violate the rights of human beings.

There is one way that what appears to be complicity could be justified: if the gains made from it are substantially devoted to, among other goals, altering or reforming the situation for the better—to fighting the policies that violate individual rights. Those who did business in the old South Africa were exonerated if they also seriously contributed to abolishing apartheid.

The bottom line is that, if businesses embark on commerce that involves unethical elements, they must make up for it by contributing to the abolition of those elements. Without that their hands are seriously tainted. For although it is morally proper for people in business to focus on prosperity, it is not right to lose sight of other moral considerations.

What this conclusion says about diplomacy toward countries with official policies that violate basic human morality and justice, too, is a complex issue. But there, no less than elsewhere, a basic principle cannot be escaped: A free society may not carry on diplomatically with countries that are substantially tyrannical unless in self-defense or because doing so contributes to the reduction of such tyranny or fends off the dangers they pose. One certainly may not pursue ordinarily immoral policies except in the service of moral objectives—on the model of, say, the spy or undercover police officer who feigns complicity so as to serve an overriding moral objective. Lying or cheating cannot be justified except to escape the likes of Nazis, Communists, or thugs.

All of this can get complicated, but the fundamentals—abstaining from contributing to the violation of basic individual rights—must never be lost sight of. That much can be said, I believe, most generally; the rest is impossible to address without attention to circumstances, history, and special considerations of various kinds.

■ ■ ■

I wish to express my gratitude to the Hoover Institution on War, Revolution and Peace, and its director, John Raisian, for generously supporting the publication of this work. In particular, I am indebted to Joanne and Johan Blokker for their financial support of my scholarship at the Hoover Institution. I also wish to thank the contributing authors for their cooperation, patience, and conscientiousness throughout the entire publishing process. Last, but not least, I wish to thank Pat Baker, Marshall Blanchard, and Ann Wood of the Hoover Institution Press for their tireless assistance with the completion of this volume.

The Universal Principles
of Business Ethics

Contrary to popular belief, there are universally valid principles of business ethics.[1] These principles operate everywhere in the world, and apply to international trade as well as to local business. Although skepticism about such universal principles of business ethics is rife, it results largely from confusions about the nature of business, ethics, and business ethics. When these basic concepts are properly understood, it can be seen that the diversity and complexity of actual circumstances, and the varied tastes and values that undeniably obtain in different parts of the world, are perfectly compatible with universal principles of business ethics.

The universal principles of business ethics can be usefully incorporated into an Ethical Decision Model, which can help business people to resolve the moral problems they confront when doing business in exotic as well as in familiar locations. By making it clear that business has an ethical infrastructure, the

    1. This chapter calls upon material first presented in Elaine Sternberg, "Relativism Rejected: The Possibility of Transnational Business Ethics" in W. Michael Hoffman et al., eds., *Emerging Global Business Ethics* (Westport, Conn.: Quorum Books, 1994), pp. 143–50; in Elaine Sternberg, *Just Business: Business Ethics in Action* (London: Little, Brown & Co., 1994); and in Elaine Sternberg, "Ethics in the Balance," *Global Custodian*, summer 1997, pp. 48–58.

Ethical Decision Model can also clarify the correct way to deal with disorderly jurisdictions and pariah regimes.

Sources of Skepticism

Cultural Relativism

It is undoubtedly true that notions of acceptable business conduct vary widely across national boundaries. The "descent from heaven"[2] that senior Japanese regard as their normal pension provision, and as a proper expression of traditional respect for age and experience, looks like avuncularism and a source of conflict of interest to the West. What northern Europe and North America castigate as bribery and corruption is the normal way of prioritizing and facilitating transactions in substantial parts of the Third World. And the interest that the West considers to be the normal fee for the rental of money is condemned by fundamentalist Islam as usury.

What constitutes acceptable business conduct also differs within the West. The American and British democratic preference for "one share one vote" is not shared by the French, who allocate additional votes to shares held for longer periods. As recently as 1994, insider trading continued to be legal in Germany, despite having been ruled out in the United States in the 1930s and having been illegal in Britain since the 1980s. In France, bribes are still not officially considered to be a misuse of corporate funds.[3]

Even within a single country, acceptable business practices can vary dramatically. The norms of Wall Street are not those of

2. *Amakudari.*
3. David Buchan, "Bribes not 'misuse of money,'" *Financial Times*, 8 February 1997, p. 2.

Main Street. What is taken for granted in Silicon Valley may seem alien in the Rust Belt. And conduct that is encouraged in a lawyer is typically denounced in a banker or a pharmaceutical company executive. Such variations in practice often raise doubts about the possibility of universal principles of business ethics.

That skepticism has been underpinned by a variety of pernicious intellectual fashions. One is the notion that business ethics is an American invention, with no relevance outside of the United States. This is a view put forward both by non-Americans who regard business ethics as an unacceptable foreign imposition, and by Americans who fear being the bearers of an imperialist doctrine. It also gains some credence from the fact that business ethics as an industry is indeed a largely American phenomenon. A series of major scandals, followed by legislation,[4] led to official ethics programs and the employment of "ethics officers" becoming a prudential requirement for much of American business. Reflecting that domestic concern, the majority of books and courses on business ethics are written by and for Americans. Such works use predominantly American language and examples to make their characteristically American points; those points, in turn, tend to reflect American preoccupations, including the political correctness that has corrupted much of American society in the last decade.

That the business ethics industry is American, however, does not mean that business ethics is. In order for business ethics to be American, two further conditions would have to be satisfied. First, what is offered in the name of "business ethics" by the American business ethics industry would have to represent all

4. Notably the Federal Sentencing Guidelines of 1991, which made having a formal business ethics program a defense against, and thus a source of lower penalties for, various federal charges, including fraud.

that is properly meant by "business ethics." In fact, quite the opposite is true: far from exhausting the subject, what is characteristically presented in the name of "business ethics" by American ethicists[5] has little to do with either business or ethics.

Even if it did, the second condition for inferring from an American business ethics industry to business ethics' being American would still not be satisfied. Contrary to what is assumed by such an inference, the truth of an intellectual discipline is independent of the identity of those who promote and teach it. Some disciplines, of course, like some games (baseball and cricket, for example) are historically associated with particular nationalities. There are even ways of conducting both games and intellectual pursuits that are associated with notional national characteristics. But the definitive contents of both are necessarily nationality-independent.

It is noteworthy that although cross-cultural differences have always existed, their tendency to undermine belief in universal values is a relatively modern phenomenon. The Greeks were supremely confident that their values were superior to all others; the term they used to denote those who did not speak their language—"barbarian"—is now a synonym for a savage. The Romans imposed their ways on most of the known world with military force and educational zeal. The British empire was built by men who dutifully shouldered the "white man's burden" to extend the benefits of civilization to unfortunate folk who lacked them, and consequently were to be pitied.

It is only in the past fifty years or so that cultural differences have routinely been associated with cultural relativism, which is the view that no one culture is any better, or any worse, than any

---

5. Who rightly avoid, because they do not deserve, the label "moral philosophers."

other.[6] Cultural relativism has stemmed partly from a revulsion against authoritarianism. Regrettably, some of the world's most repressive regimes have been based on claims to absolute truth; tyrants have often claimed ethical as well as military superiority. Seeking to combat Fascist and Communist authoritarianism, prominent advocates of the free society[7] have responded by attacking the notion of absolute truth. But though the objective is laudable, the strategy is misguided, and the target mistaken: protecting liberty requires limiting the use of coercive force, not denying the possibility of truth. Tolerance is perfectly compatible with absolute truth and absolute values, so long as those truths and values are not forcibly imposed.

Another source of cultural relativism was the 1960s revolt against received values of all sorts, especially within free societies. Reacting against a provincialism that ignored or undervalued different ways of life, and against military attempts to impose those values abroad, 1960s radicals indiscriminately rejected all received wisdom, particularly that which claimed any superiority for Western ways. Campaigns to achieve equal rights for racial minorities and women further attacked traditional assumptions. These trends, reinforced by permissive education, combined to undermine belief in all absolute values.

Cultural relativism has thus become very widespread, and has fostered a general unwillingness to make or accept universal pronouncements, including ones about business ethics. To some extent this reflects an appropriate diffidence. If business ethics were nothing but the assertion of a personal or a national preference, or a codification of local practice, then claims of univer-

6. Though ironically, and irrationally, the term is often associated with the view that Western culture, particularly as expressed in the United States, is distinctly worse than all the others, which are variously praised for being purer or more natural.

7. Notably Professor Sir Karl Popper.

sality would indeed be presumptuous. But however becoming such diffidence might be, it should nevertheless not extend to doubting the possibility of transnational business ethics: the fact that it does, reflects fundamental confusions about knowledge and business, ethics and business ethics.

Philosophical Relativism

The most fundamental confusion underlying skepticism concerning universal business ethics is philosophical skepticism about the possibility of knowledge of any sort: if the world cannot be known, neither can ethical truths about it. Such doubts have been expressed throughout the history of philosophy; the doctrine of skepticism indeed takes its name from the Greek Skeptics. In its pervasive modern form, however, generalized doubt is a legacy of Descartes. Though Descartes himself was left in no doubt, thanks to the saving grace of God, few philosophers since him have been confident of the existence of a world outside their own minds. Even when they have regained some notion of an external world, it has been too attenuated to sustain objective knowledge or, a fortiori, ethical knowledge: theories that cannot comfortably accommodate bodies have little hope of making sense of human action or of ethics.[8]

Because they lack an adequate ontology, both of the most prominent modern ethical theories—Kantian deontology and Utilitarianism—are conspicuously unable to give satisfactory accounts of ordinary ethical judgments.[9] If (counterfactually) being good simply means acting so as to maximize utility, or acting in

---

8. For an investigation of how Aristotelian naturalism avoids those fundamental problems, see Elaine Sternberg, *The Logical Conditions of Public Experience*, Ph.D. thesis, London School of Economics, University of London, 1976.

9. For an analysis of the metaphysical shortcomings of modern ethical theories, see Alasdair MacIntyre, *After Virtue: A Study in Moral Theory* (London: Gerald Duckworth & Co. Ltd., 1981).

a way that is universalizable, most common ethical judgments cannot be justified. Justice, for example, is reduced to mere utility or procedure; there is no room for the notions of merit and desert that are commonly and rightly associated with the term. Equally, such theories cannot accommodate the fact that context is relevant to moral judgments without reducing ethics to relativism or consequentialism.

In the absence of an appropriate philosophical foundation, ethical statements cannot be objectively ranked; there is no reason why any one statement should be preferred to any other. If ethical statements are no more than expressions of taste or preference, their truth becomes wholly relative to the person making them. The statement "Murder is wrong," made by Smith, reduces to "Smith believes murder is wrong," or "Smith dislikes murder."

Restoring Certainty

Establishing the possibility of objective knowledge is an essential philosophical project, and one that can be successfully accomplished.[10] It is, however, necessarily beyond the scope of this short paper. Fortunately, it also is one that need not be undertaken here: most business people do not suffer from philosophical skepticism. They do not doubt that their colleagues or their desks are real.

Popular skepticism about the possibility of universal business ethics is more likely to stem from a failure to distinguish three things that business people do encounter in their daily lives: (1) decisions about what actually should be done in particular circumstances, (2) the codification of circumstantial prece-

10. See, for example, David J. Weissman, *Truth's Debt to Value* (New Haven, Conn.: Yale University Press, 1993).

dents and rules of thumb, and (3) the basic principles underlying ethical decisions. Although specific decisions and moral codes do vary widely, basic principles do not. Clarification about the nature of ethics and ethical principles, and about the operation of rules and the nature of business, can do much to demonstrate that variations in practice neither require nor justify relativism about business ethics.

The first thing to note is that the term "ethics" is typically used to refer to a variety of different things. Sometimes it refers to moral codes and/or the actions enjoined by them. At other times, it is used to refer to principles and/or to the study of philosophical doctrines. When dealing with received opinion, such common usages will be observed, both with respect to "ethics" and "business ethics." When strictly used, however, the term "ethics" refers properly to a subsection of philosophy, that which seeks to identify and clarify the presuppositions of human conduct having to do with good and evil. Business ethics is the application of ethics to, or in, specifically business situations and activities.

Like defending objective knowledge, establishing the foundations of ethics from first principles is necessarily outside the scope of this paper: the grounds of ethical activity, like the existence of business, must here be taken as given. Certain implications of the philosophical nature of ethics are, however, crucial to the question of universality. The most important is that, as a purely theoretical[11] discipline, ethics has no necessary connection to any existing system of religious belief, or any specific legal framework, or any particular moral code. As a result, many commonly cited variations of actual practice are simply irrelevant to the question of whether there are universal truths of business

---

11. As distinct from practical.

ethics: cultural diversity, even cultural relativism, does not and cannot justify ethical relativism.

Although ethics is essentially theoretical, there is nevertheless a metaphorical sense in which the techniques and principles of ethics proper can nevertheless be helpful in dealing with real life problems. Ethics can be of practical use insofar as the clarity of thought and awareness of key concepts developed in philosophical study help to inform action. It is in this extended sense that one may properly speak of "applied ethics," or the "application" of ethics to business, or of ethics "enjoining" specific courses of action.

Business ethics is simply the application of general moral principles to specifically business situations and activities. The function of business ethics is to resolve or at least to clarify the moral issues that typically arise in business: starting from an analysis of the nature and presuppositions of business, business ethics applies general moral principles in an attempt to identify what is right.

The Nature of Principles

The universality of business ethics depends on the status of the ethical principles employed: if they are universal, then so is it. The principles of business ethics identify the ethical conditions that must obtain for business as an activity to be possible. Because they are derived from the essential nature of business, the principles apply to business whenever and wherever it is pursued. Moreover, principles are universal by their very nature. That which is not universal may be a useful rule of thumb, or a practical guideline, or a summary of common practice, but cannot be a principle. And that is because the point of principles, including moral principles, is precisely that they should identify the unvarying, essential features of diverse situations, and thus provide a unifying framework that can make sense of actual problems as they arise in all their unpredictable variety and complexity.

This accords with our ordinary understanding of morality. Ethical values are widely expected to transcend specific interests, be they national or cultural or economic; business ethics is expected to provide a basis for assessing and guiding business conduct wherever it may occur. Just as money, by providing a common standard of financial value, permits making trade-offs between items as diverse as Apple computers and apple pies, so principles, by constituting constant points of reference, make discussion and decision-making possible across widely different situations. Unlike assertions of mere preference, moral principles provide a criterion of acceptable business behavior that can be argued for, and applied consistently over a wide range of actual people, places, and times. So principles are essential: without them one might have statements of intent, or descriptions of preferred practice, but not business ethics.

Unlike preferences, principles can be evaluated and ranked. Despite the relativist claims that no one's ideas on anything are any better or worse than anyone else's, it is not the case that all views, even moral views, are equally correct. On the contrary, starting with a philosophical understanding of the nature of man and the world,[12] it is possible to abstract out ethical principles that can be seen to be genuinely better than the alternatives at making sense of the moral universe, and that do indeed express eternal verities.

Lying, cheating, and stealing are simply wrong. So are killing and cowardice, irresponsibility, breaking promises, and betrayal. Justice and fairness, in contrast, are always right, as is honesty.

12. For the philosophical framework drawn upon here, see the collected works of Aristotle, especially the *Nicomachean Ethics, The Metaphysics, The Politics, De Anima*, and the *Posterior Analytics*.

Whether or not they are actually observed or enforced, these values hold good everywhere, be it in love or war, business or pleasure . . . Africa or Asia. These values may of course not always be easily reconcilable, and hard choices may have to be made among them; given the complexities of moral life, it may sometimes be necessary to forgo one moral value in favor of another. But the value forgone remains a value nonetheless: the need to rank values never transforms virtues into vices . . . or *vice versa*.

Unlike simple assertions of taste, systems and principles can be ranked on the basis of their explanatory ability. A system that nullifies the very phenomena it sets out to clarify, as, for example, the reduction of values to mere preferences does, is less than satisfactory;[13] to be taken seriously, it would have to prove that nothing better were possible. Principles that satisfy the reality test can be further assessed in respect of their consistency, simplicity, power, and elegance: the best ethical system will be applicable everywhere and always, independent of geographical and cultural as well as temporal divides.

How can the genuinely differing tastes and attitudes that prevail worldwide be reconciled with such universal principles? Easily. First, practice may deviate from principle because the principles may simply not have been employed: philosophy cannot rule out either hypocrisy, ignorance or error, knavery or foolishness. Unlike physical laws, moral principles can be violated,[14] and sadly, they often are: rules are flouted or forgotten or misapplied and people just do behave badly.

Second, even when principles are applied correctly, out-

13. Though it is not, in the history of philosophy, at all uncommon. The Aristotelian concern for "saving the appearances" is an expression of logical rigor, not conservative prejudice.
14. Though not with moral impunity.

comes will necessarily vary: when a constant rule is applied to different inputs, different outputs are the natural result. Consider a nonmoral example. It is a basic principle of physics that every action has an equal and opposite reaction. Accordingly, action A generates reaction −A and action B, reaction −B. No one imagines, however, that because the principle is universal, that −B and −A are thereby the same. Nor do they suppose, because they are different, either that the principle has not applied or that it is any less universal. In like fashion, moral principles applied to differing circumstances naturally produce diverse results.

The Variety of Questions

Another reason that ethical judgments vary is because they are actually responses to different questions. A major confusion promoting relativism concerning universal business ethics is the failure to recognize that the question "Is business ethical?" can refer to at least three quite different inquiries: Is business being conducted ethically? Is the activity of business itself ethical? Is it ethical for a particular individual to engage in business either at all or at a given time?

The first question, concerning how to conduct business ethically, is the central issue of business ethics. It explores ethical issues that arise within the activity of business, and investigates what business must do to be ethical. Answering this question involves judging the conduct of businesses, and of people in their business capacities, against the universal principles of business ethics.

The second question concerns the moral status of the business objective itself. It is typically the question raised by those who disapprove of business and capitalism. As the Introduction to this volume points out, critics of business and free markets often assume that the activity of maximizing owner value is intrinsically immoral. Insofar as refuting that mistaken view requires analyzing the nature of the business objective, and using it to rebut common assumptions about greed, expediency, opportunism, and so on, answering this question[15] also calls upon the universal principles of business ethics.

Thoroughly defending the business objective against charges of immorality, however, requires very much more. It involves justifying maximizing and owning and value. It requires investigating, among much else, the meaning of merit and desert and entitlement, and the grounds of equality, liberty, and property.[16] These are fundamental questions, which necessarily involve going beyond the bounds of business and business ethics; analyzing such issues is a central task of ethics itself.[17]

Answering the third question—whether engaging in business is ethical for a particular individual at a given time—also requires going beyond the bounds of business ethics. However unexceptionable business is intrinsically, it may nevertheless be unethical for a particular individual to engage in or pursue business if doing so would conflict with his other, prior commitments. This is the point being made in the Introduction to this volume, when the charge of "tunnel vision" is raised. Determin-

15. Which is therefore addressed in Sternberg, *Just Business*: "Charges of Intrinsic Business Immorality Refuted," pp. 57–61.

16. For a contractarian attempt to provide such a fundamental analysis, see Jan Narveson, "Deserving Profits" in M. J. Rizzo and R. Cowan, *Profits and Morality* (Chicago: University of Chicago Press, 1995), pp. 48–87.

17. The reason why this (and the next) question cannot be answered by business ethics is because they are "meta-business" questions. Questions about the ethical status of the business purpose, and the relationship of the business purpose to other purposes, logically require going beyond the business purpose itself; they can only be answered by reference to some broader, more comprehensive end. Business ethics, in contrast, assumes the business purpose, and deals with the ethical problems that arise within the activity of business. The inability of business ethics to justify the business objective reflects a logical limitation, not any ethical failure of business or free markets.

ing whether and when business is an appropriate end to be sought requires evaluating the business objective against the variety of human objectives and values. That business may be the wrong activity for a particular individual to pursue at a specific time, however, does not mean that business is intrinsically unethical or that business cannot be conducted ethically. Nor does it count against there being universally applicable principles of business ethics. The answers are different, because they are responses to different questions.

The Irrelevance of Motives

Yet another source of skepticism about the universality of business ethics principles is a failure to understand the nature and role of motives. Confusing motives and objectives often leads people to deny that business has a single definitive objective. Pointing to the undeniable variety of factors that motivate business people, skeptics question the legitimacy of defining business exclusively in terms of a single end, and of using that end to identify universally applicable principles of business ethics.

The way to sort out these confusions is to clarify the difference between objectives and motives. The objective of an activity is ordinarily the outcome or change in circumstances that the activity is meant to achieve. Objectives typically serve to specify the identity of activities. When, for example, a man runs down the street, his physical movements are compatible with a variety of activities: he might be catching a bus or pursuing a thief or just taking exercise. It is his objective that determines which activity is involved.

Motives, in contrast, are the personal, typically emotional, impulses that prompt individuals to act; they normally characterize the way in which acts are performed. Although some objectives (e.g., healing) are conventionally associated with certain motives (benevolence), the connection is wholly contingent. The same motive is compatible with a variety of purposes, and can inspire a variety of activities: benevolence can prompt donating money to charity and excusing mistakes as well as practicing medicine. Conversely, the same objective can be pursued with a variety of motives; people can be prompted to become doctors by avarice and ambition as well as by altruism. Regardless of the motives that inspire individual physicians, however, the activity of medicine always has the same purpose: (roughly) maximizing physical well-being by preventing and curing disease.

The purpose of an activity is independent of the motives that prompt people to engage in it. The undoubted variety of human motivation is, accordingly, no obstacle to an activity's having a single, essential purpose. That people go into and conduct business for all sorts of different reasons other than accumulating wealth—for example, to exercise their talents, to carry on family traditions, to eclipse their rivals—in no way undermines business's having a definitive objective.

The Fundamental Principles of Business Ethics

Maximizing Owner Value

Understanding that business has a single, definitive objective is crucial to appreciating how there can be universal principles of business ethics. The principles of business ethics apply to business in all of its manifestations, because the principles relate to the nature of business, and that nature is invariant. Notwithstanding the multifarious forms of commercial organization found worldwide, ranging from the corner lemonade stand to the multinational corporation to the Japanese *keiretsu*, business is a single, distinct activity, differentiated from all others by its objective.

The specific objective that is unique to business, and that distinguishes business from everything else, is maximizing owner value over the long term by selling goods or services.[18] Actual commercial enterprises, of course, often do much else: they collect taxes and support charities and constitute social environments. But it is only in virtue of maximizing long-term owner value that they can be recognized as businesses. It is the objective of maximizing long-term owner value that differentiates a business from a village fête or a family, a government or a game, a profitable hobby or a commercially successful club.

Understood in this way, business is both very specific and very limited. It is not, for example, the purpose of business *qua* business to act as a social club, a school, or a charity, or to promote moral or other values. Accordingly, a business will not, except incidentally, be pursuing social welfare or spiritual development or psychic gratification. That these highly variable ends are irrelevant for business is one main reason why cultural diversity has no bearing on the universal validity of business ethics principles.

The principles of business ethics are simply those that are presupposed by the definitive business activity: maximizing long-term owner value by selling goods or services. Long-term views require confidence in a future, and confidence requires trust. Accordingly, the conditions of trust must be observed. Equally, owner value presupposes ownership and therefore respect for property rights. In order not to be ultimately self-defeating, business must therefore be conducted with honesty, fairness, the absence of physical violence and coercion, and a

---

18. For a full explanation, justification and application of this notion of business, see Sternberg, *Just Business*, especially chapter 2. "Business" will be used here exclusively to designate the activity of maximizing long-term owner value by selling goods or services, and, by extension, the associations pursuing it.

presumption in favor of legality. Collectively, these constraints embody what may be called *"ordinary decency."*

Furthermore, since business is more likely to achieve its definitive purpose when it encourages contributions to that purpose, and not to some other, classical *"distributive justice"* is also essential. Just as "ordinary decency" is distinct from vague notions of "niceness," this concept of justice has nothing to do with modern attempts to redistribute income on ideological grounds. What distributive justice requires is simply that within an organization, contributions to the organizational objective be the basis for distributing organizational rewards: those who do most for the organization deserve most from the organization. Though the term "distributive justice" may be unfamiliar, the underlying concept is widely recognized. It is implicit in the commonly accepted view that productive workers deserve more than shirkers; when properly structured, both performance-related pay and promotion on merit are expressions of distributive justice.

Distributive Justice

Distributive justice is an extremely powerful concept: it allows for the full range of divergent human purposes, and for rewards as diverse as payments and praise, honors and responsibilities. Distributive justice serves both as a principle of allocation and as a principle of selection. Distributive justice governs more than just remuneration. It also determines who should be hired and fired, and which bidders should be awarded contracts, and even, by extension, which products and plants and projects should be financed.

The principle of distributive justice is so fundamental that it is important to avert a number of potential misunderstandings. First, what is relevant for judgments of distributive justice is not the nature of the contributor—his identity or his motives—but only the contribution itself. Distributive justice is concerned essentially with achievements; dispositions and aspirations are relevant to businesses only insofar as they actually or potentially affect long-term owner value.

Second, because distributive justice relates only to contributions, it is wrong to extend its judgments to cover the characters or capabilities or general worth of the contributors. When, in a business, distributive justice decrees that A is more deserving than B of a pay raise or a promotion, it does not necessarily imply that A is morally superior, or a better person; it simply means that A has made the greater contribution to maximizing long-term owner value.

Third, what is fair or just according to distributive justice is always relative to the defining purpose of a particular organization, not to some abstract, external standard. Distributive justice is not about some notional "just wage" or "fair price" or "appropriate return." Furthermore, distributive justice specifies only the relative, and not the absolute, rewards to be allotted. The basic unit of reward will vary from organization to organization, and within each organization will vary over time depending on the organization's circumstances.

Finally, distributive justice does not require equal treatment for everyone with the same job description. Quite the reverse: the principle of distributive justice asserts that those who contribute more deserve more. Such contributions are, however, a matter of actual achievement, not administrative category. There are typically wide variations in performance within any personnel classification, while those with different job titles may well make contributions of equal worth. The best manager contributes more than the worst manager; the worst manager may well contribute less than the best secretary. "Equal pay for equal work" in business expresses distributive justice only if the work is equated on the basis of its contribution to long-term owner value.

Ordinary Decency

Nevertheless, "treating equals equally" is indeed a requirement of business ethics: it is part of what is meant by fairness, and as such is a component of ordinary decency. Like distributive justice, however, the components of ordinary decency need clarification if they are not to be misconstrued. Ordinary decency consists of fairness and honesty and refraining from coercion and physical violence, typically within the confines of the law.

While fairness requires "treating equals equally," it does not mean treating everyone, even everyone in the business, alike. Not all ways of being equal are relevant to the business objective, or deserve equal treatment by the business. People may well be equal in respect of their hair color, but the business need not treat all redheads in the same way to be fair. What "treating equals equally" does require is simply that insofar as the organization has rules, it should apply them systematically and evenhandedly, without favor or capricious exception.

Fairness also requires honoring agreements. The ethical business scrupulously performs its part of the bargain when it enters into contracts, whether they are explicit and written or implicit and based purely on trust. In order for arrangements based on trust to work satisfactorily, however, all the parties need to have the same understanding of the arrangements they have made. The ethical business is therefore extremely careful about the expectations that it engenders or allows to arise about it; inappropriate expectations are a major source of the perception that business is unfair. The ethical business does not encourage or condone unrealistic expectations about its activities, objectives, or abilities. And it is equally careful to fulfill the realistic expectations that it has fostered, not disappointing them without good reason and good explanation.

Honesty also requires clarification. In business as elsewhere, being honest means being accurate in description and keeping one's word, both when that word is enshrined in contract and otherwise. Contrary to widespread belief, however, failing to tell "the truth, the whole truth, and nothing but the truth" is not necessarily dishonest. "The truth, the whole truth, and nothing but the truth" is the standard that applies to testimony in a court of law. Even there, however, its application is limited: witnesses can only answer questions put to them by counsel. To expect the legal standard of truthfulness to apply in other situations is seriously inappropriate; it is normally a mark of social ineptitude or deliberate provocation. Just as context and purpose are crucial in determining utterances' meaning and the appropriate responses to them, they are equally essential in determining what counts as honesty. Sales pitches and advertising are not dishonest because they fail to provide impartial consumer advice: that is simply not their function.

The key to business ethics is very simple: *business is ethical when it maximizes long-term owner value subject to distributive justice and ordinary decency*. If an organization is not directed at maximizing long-term owner value, it is not a business; if it does not pursue that definitive business purpose with distributive justice and ordinary decency, it is not ethical. The essential nature of business and the principles of business ethics are universals that are unaffected by circumstantial differences.

The Ethical Decision Model

The universal principles of business ethics can be incorporated into an Ethical Decision Model. The Ethical Decision Model identifies which problems businessmen actually need to address in their business capacities, and offers a way to resolve them. The Model indicates what information is relevant to ethical decision-making. It organizes that information so that it will be more productive in leading to a decision. It specifies the ethical principles to be employed in deciding what is right. The Model introduces conceptual clarity and structure to matters that are too often clouded by emotion and moral fervor. It thereby provides a way of managing and resolving ethical problems in business.

The Ethical Decision Model consists of four straightforward steps.

Step 1: Clarify the Question

The critically important first step in tackling all issues of business ethics is clarifying exactly what is at issue. In the forms in which they are commonly posed—by the media, by demanding interest groups, by disgruntled stakeholders—ethical questions often seem perplexing, either trivial or intractable. One reason why the answers frequently seem so elusive is because, in many cases, the questions themselves are fatally flawed. Like "When did you stop beating your wife?" many questions of business ethics need to be unpacked before they can be sensibly answered. Failure to separate out the different matters at issue is a major source of confusion in resolving ethical questions, both in business and elsewhere.

Step 2: Determine Its Relevance for This Business

Having analyzed the issue, the second step is to determine whether the question that remains actually is a problem for this business; if it is not, then there is no business ethics issue for this business to resolve. The inquiry has three parts: Is the issue relevant to *business*? Is it relevant to *this* business? And is it a *problem* for this business?

The first question is the most basic: Does the issue relate to maximizing long-term owner value? Unless it does, there is no business concern at issue, and nothing to be evaluated in terms of distributive justice and ordinary decency. Even if a concern is relevant to business, it must still be determined whether it is relevant to this business, and whether it represents a problem for it. If the answer is easy and obvious, or prescribed by law, there will generally not be an ethical problem to be resolved.

Step 3: Identify the Circumstantial Constraints

Once the relevance of the question has been established, the next step is to identify the constraints that may limit solutions. Business decisions are constrained not only by law and regulation, but also by contractual, cultural, economic, physical, and technical considerations. Even though the principles of ethical conduct are constant over time and place and industry, what businesses actually can do is crucially affected by their individual circumstances.

Step 4: Assess the Available Options

The fourth step is to see how alternative solutions measure up against maximizing long-term owner value and respecting distributive justice and ordinary decency.

Assessing a proposal's potential effect on long-term owner value is a straightforward business calculation. All significant potential costs and consequences, including those that are distant and delayed and indirect, must be weighed against all the potential benefits. The judgments of distributive justice and ordinary decency which a business must make are, in comparison, reasonably simple; unlike assessments of owner value, they are not normally ones of degree or extent. Alternatives either do, or do not, satisfy the conditions; those which do not are not ethical for the business.

Conclusion: The Right Course of Action

Once the relevant questions and constraints have been identified, and alternative proposals have been assessed, the ethical answer should be clear. The business should choose that alternative which is likely to contribute most to long-term owner value, so long as it satisfies distributive justice and ordinary decency. If either of those conditions is not met, then even if the proposal appears to maximize long-term owner value, it should not be adopted. But equally, satisfying distributive justice and ordinary decency is not enough. The morally right course of action for the business must satisfy all three requirements: it is that which aims at maximizing long-term owner value *while* respecting distributive justice and ordinary decency.

Typically, the hardest part of ethical decision-making is not applying the principles of distributive justice and ordinary decency, but determining which action will actually maximize long-term owner value. But however difficult it may be to project outcomes, estimating long-term owner value cannot be avoided: it is the core not just of ethical decision-making, but of business as such.

Applications

"Good Ethics Is Good Business"

Understanding business and business ethics in this way should help to make the universality of the principles of business ethics more plausible. It should also help to overcome one of the fundamental obstacles to business acceptance of business ethics: the mistaken notion that business ethics is necessarily inimical to business. It does so in three ways. First, when business ethics is properly understood, it becomes clear that it has nothing to do with unproductive "do-gooding." Quite the contrary: business ethics positively requires that owner value be maximized, subject only to respecting distributive justice and ordinary decency. Second, those values are not incompatible with business operations:

they are necessary for business's existence as an activity. Finally, what business has to maximize is not current-period accounting profits but long-term owner value. Unlike short-term profits, owner value necessarily reflects the indirect, distant, and qualitative effects of a business's actions. When, therefore, business is understood as maximizing long-term owner value, it becomes entirely plausible that business performance should be enhanced by ethical conduct.

While it is generally true that "good ethics is good business," it is nevertheless important to recognize the limitations of that slogan. It does not mean that ethical conduct is the same thing as business success, or that the one guarantees the other. If a lucrative but illegal contract has to be refused, or honesty costs the business an important transaction, acting ethically can lead to business losses. Doing the right thing can sometimes cost dearly; business success does not follow automatically from acting ethically. Conversely, business success is no guarantee of ethical conduct. At least in the short run, spectacular rewards can sometimes result from doing the wrong thing, in business as elsewhere. But while it may be disturbing to see the wicked prosper, their doing so does not undermine the moral basis of business ethics; that relies neither on the ability of ethical conduct to generate business success, nor on a cost-benefit analysis. "Good ethics is good business" is simply an observation about business ethics, not a moral justification of it.

Bribery

The Ethical Decision Model can do much to illuminate bribery, an issue that is often used to challenge the existence of universal principles of business ethics. First, it encourages clarification of exactly what is involved. A bribe is an incentive offered to encourage someone to break the rules of the organization he nominally represents and deliver an (unfairly) favorable outcome. Although commonly associated with governments and the third world, bribery is a problem that can equally afflict private organizations and all locales. The defense contractor greasing the palm of an official in order to secure a government contract is guilty of bribery, but so too is the leisure group giving travel agents free holidays to skew their clients' custom.

Bribery is not involved when local principles are duly observed, and rewards are allocated in accordance with the local rules. If, for example, goods are officially allocated on the basis of the highest payment received, what is involved is not bribery but an auction. The local system might perhaps allocate goods on the basis of their effect on family influence, or power, or prestige. When that is so, even ostensibly commercial transactions may well be conducted on the basis of contributions to those nonbusiness ends. In such circumstances, bribery may not be involved, but maximizing long-term owner value will still be problematical. Not only may benefits due to the business be difficult to identify and enforce, but if what is done even *looks* like bribery, it may well, albeit unjustly, diminish both the briber's and the bribed's reputation with those who find bribery objectionable.

Wherever bribery does occur, it is wrong. That is because bribery violates distributive justice: by hypothesis, the benefit (for example, the contract to do the business, the access to confidential information) is awarded in exchange for the bribe, instead of on the relevant merits of the case. Damaging conflict of interest[19] is an essential feature of bribery: the individual or group that is bribed receives the benefit of the bribe, but it is the organization that is expected to deliver the goods . . . typically in ways that are contrary to its best interests. Even if the bribe-

---

19. For an analysis of conflicts of interest, and how to handle them ethically, see Sternberg, *Just Business*, especially pp. 100–104.

induced end would have been the one coming about in the ordinary course of events, bribery would still be wrong: it would violate ordinary decency, because the bribed would have lied and cheated about the benefits they were purporting to provide.

Bribes are also wrong for those who offer them, the bribers: by definition, they are attempts to cheat. Where corruption is endemic, bribery may perhaps seem the only way to proceed. Even then, however, the question is not whether circumstances can make bribery right: they cannot.[20] The proper question instead is whether those are appropriate markets or countries or societies in which to be attempting business. That is a question that will be addressed at some length below, in the section "Dealing with Disorderly Jurisdictions."

Exploiting Lower Standards Abroad

Consider another issue often cited against universal principles of business ethics: is it ethical for a manufacturer to sell elsewhere products that fail to meet the standards of its sophisticated home market? The answer is simple: it is ethical if it maximizes owner value while respecting distributive justice and ordinary decency. When the differing standards reflect differences of taste, or of wealth, there is no obvious reason why satisfying them would be not ethical: it is a mark of the successful marketeer to fulfill the needs of his customers. If the target market is too poor to afford color televisions, it is good business, not moral condescension, to offer black and white sets instead . . . even if they would not sell well in the United States. And it is wise to remember that standards that the selling market considers higher may not be regarded as such by the buyers: the automatic

---

20. Even when, in extreme circumstances, bribery may be necessary to avert a greater evil, and thus is the right thing to do in the circumstances, it remains wrong in itself: the lesser evil is still an evil.

transmission that the U.S. driver expects as standard equipment is rejected disparagingly by most European motorists.

What about cases when the target market is genuinely less sophisticated, and the manufacturer is dumping products that can no longer be sold at home because they are considered unsafe or somehow defective? If the danger is small, and does not violate the requirements of distributive justice or ordinary decency, then what should be done depends on what will maximize owner value. The car without seat belts that may not be sold in Britain may be sold legally and profitably in the Third World, where it is regarded as a positive boon. Similarly, the lives of starving people overseas can be profitably saved by food that is wholesome past its British "sell by" date.

If the products are seriously unsafe, however, then it would be a violation of ordinary decency to sell them in any market. It would also be counterproductive. The electric teakettle that is prone to electrocute its user is more likely to attract costly prosecutions and distrust than profitable repeat business. Similarly, if the danger is such that, although not obvious, it is inescapable, then sales will continue only at everyone's peril. If the pollutants will poison everyone's atmosphere, then it is not in the long-term best interest of the business to sell the product anywhere.

Although short-term profits may be available, the business must weigh them against present and future consequences. Costs will likely result in the long term, when perceptions in the foreign market catch up with those at home. But costs may be substantial well before then, as the home market reacts to the business's questionable policies abroad. If the products are deemed dangerous, even when far away, then disapproving stakeholders are likely to vote with their feet: the business whose ethics are thought dubious may well find it harder to attract employees or suppliers or finances.

International Investment

The Ethical Decision Model can also illuminate the ethical status of international investment. Foreign investment, particularly foreign direct investment, is often deemed unethical because it alters the "natural" condition of the recipient countries or companies. And it is certainly true that foreign investment often changes local power relations, and affects the environment. But it does not follow that doing so is immoral: there is no necessary violation of either distributive justice or ordinary decency. It is equally mistaken automatically to condemn investment for undermining local customs and traditions. Investment is not forcibly imposed: normally, it is actively sought. Moreover, despite what relativists may claim, sanitation and capitalism are not mere Western values: they are genuinely better than the disease and primitive allocation systems they typically replace. Change compatible with business ethics can represent real progress.

Investment has also been denounced for the diametrically opposite reason, for failing sufficiently to alter local economic and social conditions. Business investment is not immoral because it fails to dislodge tyrannical regimes or raise the standard of living of the poorest groups. The objective of business is not creating democracy or equality. Nor does investment necessarily constitute exploitation even if standards of pay, benefits, working conditions, and worker involvement are different from those at home. Even in the developed world, employees working for the same firm often get conspicuously different working conditions and remuneration packages when they work in different countries; levels may even be different within the same country, when employees work in different departments. Such differences, however, do not necessarily mean that any of the employees have been treated unethically: more likely, they have just made different contributions to the business objective.

The Ethical Decision Model indicates why it is not the responsibility of business to improve the ethical or economic conditions of the countries in which they operate. It is because such amelioration is not normally required either to maximize owner value, or to respect distributive justice or ordinary decency. On the contrary, satisfying those three conditions may instead require investors to stay clear of disorderly regimes.

The Ethical Infrastructure of Business

Disorderly regimes are problematical for business, because business is only possible where the ethical infrastructure is as sound as the physical infrastructure. The ethical infrastructure of business is the institutional framework that must obtain for business to be possible. Whereas the principles of business ethics specify the ethical values that are presupposed by business, the ethical infrastructure consists of the institutions that are normally needed to support the operation of those values and business. Like clean air and pure water, the ethical infrastructure is so fundamental that it is normally taken for granted in well-ordered societies. In emerging markets, however, key elements of the ethical infrastructure are often missing. Since 1997, both the World Bank and the International Monetary Fund have emphasized the essential importance of the ethical infrastructure for both economic growth and the operation of capital markets.[21]

The key features of the ethical infrastructure of business are property rights and the rule of law. Property rights must be well-defined and secure. They include not just clear title to property, but the ability to exploit property, to exclude others from using it, and to transfer it, all without fear of being overridden. Property rights in turn normally require the rule of law, at very least to punish theft and violence, and to enforce contracts. The rule

---

21. "Reasons to Be Venal," *The Economist*, 16 August 1997, p. 76.

of law also means that the government and its agents, particularly the police and the judiciary, must not themselves be arbitrary or corrupt.

The importance of the ethical infrastructure can be demonstrated by considering what it is like to attempt business without it. When, for example, the rule of law is weak, both people and property are at risk of physical violence: there is a "war of all against all." In Russia, Mafia rule has increasingly replaced the rule of law, and protection rackets and extortion are rampant.[22] According to a popular local saying, "Russian law is like a lamp post: it can always be got round." Consequently, Russian business resembles Russian roulette. In Nigeria and Colombia, oil pipelines have been subject to sabotage, and oil company staff have been held hostage. In Burma, violations of people and property have been so serious that many businesses have withdrawn from the country, and sanctions have been imposed by the United States, the United Nations, and the European Union.

When property rights are not respected, investors are in danger of losing their investments. In the most extreme cases, property is lost through expropriation and extortion. Consider the compulsory "donation" of 2 percent of earnings by Indonesian companies[23] to a special government "charity." Property rights require the right to exploit as well as to hold property. When counterfeiting and piracy are tolerated (as they have been in China), investors can lose vast sums from what is effectively theft.

Enforceable shareholder rights are particularly important. Though enshrined in law, shareholder rights are not much better

---

22. Kevin Done, "Organised crime revenues at $900m," *Financial Times*, 14 April 1997, p. 3.

23. Manuela Saragosa, "Suharto seeks 2% company 'donations,'" *Financial Times*, 17 January 1996, p. 3.

respected in Russia than human rights were in the USSR. According to a 1997 study, all of Russia's 100 biggest companies have "serious problems" of corporate governance.[24] As a result, there is little shareholders can do when their companies serve traditional vested interests rather than owner value.[25]

Enforcing property rights can be a problem in even the most sophisticated markets. Britain's Commercial Union insurance company, a major institutional investor, threatened to strip shareholders of their right to vote at the Annual General Meeting. In the United States, Pennsylvania's notorious anti-takeover Act 36 of 1990 enshrines a degree of contempt for shareholder rights that Soviet *apparatchiks* would have admired. Vigilance is the price of property as well as liberty . . . everywhere and always.

Dealing with Disorderly Jurisdictions

In disorderly jurisdictions, those in which the ethical infrastructure is weak or nonexistent, the proper question is whether businesses should be operating there at all. This is also the right question to ask about operating in pariah regimes, those guilty of major violations of human rights. Like the problem "Is business ethical?" analyzed above,[26] the question "Is it ethical to conduct business in this particular jurisdiction?" typically refers to two different inquiries. There is the standard business ethics

24. Joseph Blasi, Maya Kroumova, and Douglas Krause, "Kremlin Capitalism: Privatizing the Russian Economy" (Ithaca, N.Y.: Cornell University Press, 1997); reported in John Thornhill, "Risks of Russian Market Exposed," *Financial Times*, 25 March 1997, p. 2.

25. Consider, for example, the difficulty that the shareholders of Novolipetsk Metallurgical Kombinat had in getting their company to accept new directors, conduct an audit, and cease favoring workers and directors over shareholders. John Thornhill, "Forced into a New Mould," *Financial Times*, 22 April 1997, p. 23.

26. In the section "The Variety of Questions."

question: Is it possible to conduct business ethically here? And there is also what might be called the meta-business question: Is it ethical to pursue the business objective here?

Answering the first question is a matter of determining whether it is possible to maximize owner value in the jurisdiction while also respecting distributive justice and ordinary decency. Because disorderly jurisdictions (which typically include all pariah regimes)[27] by hypothesis lack the necessary ethical infrastructure, it will be very difficult for organizations to respect distributive justice and ordinary decency while operating in them. It will also be difficult to maximize owner value. However tempting the business opportunities in disorderly jurisdictions may seem, the ability to exploit them successfully will be slim. Human rights and property rights are closely related: unless both are respected, neither is safe.

Furthermore, even the suggestion that a firm is collaborating with a repressive regime can cause both the firm itself and those associated with it to suffer financial loss. Increasingly, boycotts are directed not just at repressive regimes, but at the companies that operate in them, and even at those companies' stakeholders. Laws adopted in San Francisco and Massachusetts prohibit government contracts (including pension investment) from going to firms having even indirect connections with Burma. In Britain, protesters have targeted the Prudential Assurance Company because it owns shares of Shell, and Shell does business in Nigeria. Operating in disorderly jurisdictions and pariah regimes may give rise to short-term profits, but it seldom maximizes owner value.

Even if it did, there remains the meta-business question of whether it is ethical to pursue business in a pariah regime. That

27. Although it is theoretically possible for a pariah regime to exist in an orderly jurisdiction, mass violations of human rights have typically involved arbitrary government action and denial of property rights.

decision cannot legitimately be made by a business's executives or by its board: their authority extends at most to deciding how the business should be run, not to determining whether the firm should be a business. Deciding whether, and to what extent, the organization should be conducted as a business is instead the prerogative of the business's owners: only they have the right to subordinate the business objective to some other purpose.[28] It would be presumptuous and impertinent, and a denial of fundamental property rights, for business executives to impose their ethical or political views on the business's owners. Notwithstanding the clamorings of insistent protest groups, the wrongs of repressive jurisdictions cannot be alleviated by violating human rights elsewhere.

But how are the business owners to decide between pursuing business and boycotting or resisting pariah regimes? It is important to recognize that this is but one expression of a much more general question, "When is it right to pursue business rather than some other objective?" That query, as indicated above (in the section on The Variety of Questions), is a fundamental ethical issue. It is involved when individuals choose to devote their lives or their savings to business rather than to medicine or to gardening, as well as when they contemplate protesting against pariah regimes. Answering that question requires, among much else, ranking basic human values. It is therefore not surprising that the question seems so difficult, and that answers are so diverse.

There are, however, some considerations that are ubiquitous. Most ethical systems consider it wrong to inflict unnecessary harm, however harm is defined. Most also hold that, other things being equal, actions that inflict less harm are ethically preferable to those that inflict more harm.[29] It is therefore appropriate to

28. Though governments have the power to do so.
29. This is a view that is independent of any form of Utilitarianism, which

consider the sorts of harm that are involved in doing business in or with pariah regimes. The decision as to whether business should be pursued in such jurisdictions will depend in part on the assessment of whether operating in them is likely to do more harm than good.

Operating in pariah regimes normally harms the business owners and their stakeholders. Their characters are sullied to varying degrees through contact with corruption and complicity with the evil of violating basic human rights. Insofar as doing business with pariah regimes lends support to those regimes, by increasing their wealth or ostensible legitimacy, complicity also harms the victims of those regimes. Nevertheless, unless moral fervor is backed with careful judgment and a thorough understanding of the facts of complex situations, protests may well be ineffective in reducing that harm, or even positively counterproductive.

Boycotts against corporate investment in pariah regimes are often ineffective, because they are difficult to target precisely, and because many regimes do not care about world opinion or the condition of their own compatriots. Even when boycotts successfully reduce investment, they may make things worse for the people they are supposed to help. Eliminating "sweatshops" and child labor may force the poor into poverty and crime; prostitution may be the main alternative to destitution. Targeted projects may have beneficial effects for locals that would be lost if investment were withdrawn. Abandoned projects may harm the environment more than properly maintained ones. Resources that would have been used for the project may be freed to fund repression.

---

reduces the ethical to the greatest good for the greatest number, however the good is defined.

Campaigning for regulation is a particularly dangerous way of responding to repressive regimes. Forcibly imposed boycotts prevent consenting adults and organizations from contracting with each other; they therefore interfere with a fundamental human right. Government-enforced boycotts are typically harmful both to consumers in the home market and to producers in foreign markets; often a mask for pernicious economic protectionism, they are a major source of economic stagnation. Regulation is also often positively counterproductive: setting minimum wages notoriously destroys jobs.

An even more fundamental reason for resisting regulation as a cure is that regulation is a necessary precondition of corruption. Bending the rules is only possible—or profitable—when there are rules to be bent. Organized crime has become an international force largely because U.S. attempts to outlaw alcohol and addictive drugs have made trafficking in those substances hugely profitable. In addition, when regulation restricts normal activity, and official permissions are routinely required, bribery flourishes: it may seem the only way to get things done.

Worst of all, regulation can actually make jurisdictions less orderly. The more regulation there is, the more likely it is to be bad regulation. Some bad regulation directly constitutes a moral hazard, by creating a positive incentive to do the wrong thing. Subsidies, for example, typically encourage uneconomic operations. Moreover, many regulations cannot be enforced. Prohibitions of alcohol and drugs are notoriously ineffective. Worse still, some regulations are inherently incapable of being obeyed, because they are internally inconsistent, or contradict other regulations. When the applicable rules cannot be simultaneously heeded, people must choose which ones to obey. In the end, they may come to regard them all as optional. Bad law brings all law into contempt.

The way for a business to fulfill its moral responsibilities is not to legislate for others, but to make sure that its own conduct is ethical. That obligation applies to all business, everywhere and always, as do the principles of business ethics. The obligation for an ethical business to maximize owner value while respecting with distributive justice and ordinary decency is universal: it applies regardless of participants' race, creed, sex, or national origin, whenever and wherever business exists.

Bibliography

Aristotle. *Nicomachean Ethics, The Metaphysics, The Politics, De Anima, Posterior Analytics.*

MacIntyre, Alasdair. *After Virtue: A Study in Moral Theory.* London: Gerald Duckworth & Co. Ltd., 1981.

Narveson, Jan. "Deserving Profits." In M. J. Rizzo and R. Cowan, *Profits and Morality.* Chicago: University of Chicago Press, 1995, pp. 48–87.

Sternberg, Elaine. "Ethics in the Balance." *Global Custodian,* summer 1997.

———. *Just Business: Business Ethics in Action.* London: Little, Brown & Co., 1994.

———. "The Logical Conditions of Public Experience," Ph.D. thesis. London School of Economics, University of London, 1976.

———. "Relativism Rejected: The Possibility of Transnational Business Ethics." In W. Michael Hoffman et al., eds. *Emerging Global Business Ethics.* Westport, Conn.: Quorum Books, 1994, pp. 143–50.

Weissman, David J. *Truth's Debt to Value.* New Haven, Conn.: Yale University Press, 1993.

Human Rights and Asian Values

In 1776, just when the Declaration of Independence was being adopted in this country, Thomas Paine complained, in *Common Sense*, that Asia had "long expelled" freedom. In this lament, Paine saw Asia in company with much of the rest of the world (America, he hoped, would be different).

> Freedom hath been hunted round the globe. Asia and Africa have long expelled her. Europe regards her a stranger and England hath given her warning to depart.

For Paine, political freedom and democracy were valuable everywhere, even though they were being violated nearly everywhere too.

The violation of freedom and democracy in different parts of the world continues today, even if not as comprehensively as in Paine's time. There is a difference, though. A new class of arguments has emerged that denies the universal importance of these freedoms. The most prominent of these contentions is the claim

This essay was originally delivered as the Sixteenth Morgenthau Memorial Lecture, commissioned by the Carnegie Council on Ethics and International Affairs. The edited text was published in booklet form by the Carnegie Council, copyright © 1997. Reprinted with permission.

that Asian values do not give freedom the same importance as it is accorded in the West. Given this difference in value systems, the argument runs, Asia must be faithful to its own system of political priorities.

Cultural and value differences between Asia and the West were stressed by several official delegations at the 1993 World Conference on Human Rights in Vienna. The foreign minister of Singapore warned that "universal recognition of the ideal of human rights can be harmful if universalism is used to deny or mask the reality of diversity."[1] The Chinese delegation played a leading role in emphasizing regional differences and in making sure that the prescriptive framework adopted in the declarations made room for regional diversity. The spokesman for China's foreign ministry even put on record the proposition, apparently applicable in China and elsewhere, that "individuals must put the state's rights before their own."[2]

I shall examine the thesis that Asian values are less supportive of freedom and more concerned with order and discipline than are Western values, and that the claims of human rights in the areas of political and civil liberties are, therefore, less relevant in Asia than in the West. The defense of authoritarianism in Asia on grounds of the special nature of Asian values calls for historical scrutiny, to which I shall presently turn. But there is also a different line of justification that argues for authoritarian governance in the interest of economic development in Asia. Lee Kuan

1. Quoted in W. S. Wong, "The Real World of Human Rights" (mimeographed, 1993).

2. Quoted in John F. Cooper, "Peking's Post-Tiananmen Foreign Policy: The Human Rights Factor," *Issues and Studies* 30 (October 1994): 69; see also Jack Donnelly, "Human Rights and Asian Values," paper presented at a workshop of the Carnegie Council's Human Rights Initiative, "Changing Conceptions of Human Rights in a Growing East Asia," in Hakone, Japan, June 23–25, 1995.

Yew, the former prime minister of Singapore and a great champion of "Asian values," has defended authoritarian arrangements on the ground of their alleged effectiveness in promoting economic success. I shall consider this argument before turning to historical issues.

Asian Values and Economic Development

Does authoritarianism really work so well? It is certainly true that some relatively authoritarian states (such as South Korea, Lee's own Singapore, and post-reform China) have had faster rates of economic growth than many less authoritarian ones (including India, Costa Rica, and Jamaica). But the "Lee hypothesis" is, in fact, based on very selective information, rather than on any general statistical testing of the wide-ranging data that are available. We cannot take the high economic growth of China or South Korea in Asia as proof positive that authoritarianism does better in promoting economic growth, any more than we can draw the opposite conclusion on the basis of the fact that the fastest growing country in Africa (and one of the fastest growers in the world) is Botswana, which has been a oasis of democracy in that unhappy continent. Much depends on the precise circumstance.

There is, in fact, little general evidence that authoritarian governance and the suppression of political and civil rights are really beneficial in encouraging economic development. The statistical picture is much more complex. Systematic empirical studies give no real support to the claim that there is a conflict between political rights and economic performance.[3] The

3. See, among other studies, Robert J. Barro and Jong-Wha Lee, "Losers and Winners in Economic Growth," Working Paper 4341, National Bureau of Economic Research (1993); Partha Dasgupta, *An Inquiry into Well-Being and Desti-*

directional linkage seems to depend on many other circumstances, and while some statistical investigations note a weakly
negative relation, others find a strongly positive one. On balance,
the hypothesis that there is no relation between the two in either
direction is hard to reject. Since political liberty and individual
freedom have importance of their own, the case for them remains
untarnished.

There is also a more basic issue of research methodology
here. We must not only look at statistical connections, we must
also examine the causal processes that are involved in economic
growth and development. The economic policies and circumstances that led to the economic success of East Asian economies
are by now reasonably well understood. While different empirical studies have varied in emphasis, there is by now a fairly well-
accepted general list of "helpful policies," among them openness
to competition, the use of international markets, a high level of
literacy and school education, successful land reforms, and public provision of incentives for investment, exporting, and indus-
trialization. There is nothing whatsoever to indicate that any of
these policies is inconsistent with greater democracy and had to
be sustained by the elements of authoritarianism that happened
to be present in South Korea or Singapore or China.[4] The recent
Indian experience also shows that what is needed for generating

---

tution (Oxford: Clarendon Press, 1993); John Helliwell, "Empirical Linkages
Between Democracy and Economic Growth," Working Paper 4066, National
Bureau of Economic Research (1994); Surjit Bhalla, "Freedom and Economic
Growth: A Vicious Circle?" presented at the Nobel Symposium in Uppsala on
"Democracy's Victory and Crisis," August 1994; Adam Przeworski and Fer-
nando Limongi, "Democracy and Development," presented at the Nobel Sym-
posium in Uppsala cited above; Adam Przeworski et al., *Sustainable Democracy*
(New York: Cambridge University Press, 1995); Robert J. Barro, *Getting It Right:
Markets and Choices in a Free Society* (Cambridge, MA: MIT Press, 1996).

4. On this see also my joint study with Jean Drèze, *Hunger and Public Action*
(Oxford: Clarendon Press, 1989), Part III.

faster economic growth is a friendlier economic climate, rather than a harsher political system.

It is also important to look at the connection between political and civil rights, on the one hand, and the prevention of major disasters, on the other. Political and civil rights give people the opportunity to draw attention forcefully to general needs and to demand appropriate public action. The response of a government to acute suffering often depends on the pressure that is put on it, and this is where the exercise of political rights (voting, criticizing, protesting, and so on) can make a real difference. I have discussed elsewhere the remarkable fact that in the terrible history of famines in the world, no substantial famine has ever occurred in any independent and democratic country with a relatively free press.[5] Whether we look at famine, in Sudan, Ethiopia, Somalia, or other countries with dictatorial regimes, or in the Soviet Union in the 1930s, or in China during the period 1958 to 1961 with the failure of the Great Leap Forward (when between 23 million and 30 million people died), or currently in North Korea, we do not find exceptions to this rule.[6]

While this connection is clearest in the case of famine prevention, the positive role of political and civil rights applies to the prevention of economic and social disasters in general. When things go fine and everything is routinely good, this role of democracy may not be badly missed. It comes into its own when

5. Amartya Sen, "Development: Which Way Now?" *Economic Journal* 93 (1983) and *Resources, Values and Development* (Cambridge, MA: Harvard University Press 1984, 1997); see also Drèze and Sen, *Hunger and Public Action.*

6. Although Ireland was a part of democratic Britain during its famines of the 1840s, the extent of political dominance of London over the Irish was so strong and the social distance so great (well illustrated by Edmund Spenser's several unfriendly descriptions of the Irish as early as the sixteenth century) that the English rule of Ireland was, for all practical purposes, a colonial rule. The separation and independence of Ireland later on simply confirmed the nature of the division.

things get fouled up, for one reason or another. Then the political incentives provided by democratic governance acquire great practical value. To concentrate only on economic incentives (such as the market systems provides) while ignoring political incentives (such as democratic systems are equipped to provide) is to opt for a deeply unbalanced set of ground rules.

Asia as a Unit

I turn now to the nature of relevance of Asian values. This is not an easy exercise, for various reasons. The size of Asia, where about 60 percent of the total world population lives, is itself a problem. What can we take to be the values of so vast a region, with such diversity? There are no quintessential values that apply to this immensely large and heterogeneous population, that differentiate Asians as a group from people in the rest of the world.

The temptation to see Asia as one unit reveals, in fact, a distinctly Eurocentric perspective. Indeed, the term "the Orient," which was widely used for a long time to mean essentially what Asia means today, referred to the direction of the rising sun. It requires a heroic generalization to see such a large group of people in terms of the positional view from the European side of the Bosporus.

In practice, the advocates of "Asian values" have tended to look primarily at East Asia as the region of particular applicability. The generalization about the contrast between the west and Asia often concentrates on the land to the east of Thailand, even though there is an even more ambitious claim that the rest of Asia is also rather "similar." For example, Lee Kuan Yew outlines "the fundamental difference between Western concepts of society and government and East Asian concepts" by explaining, "When I say East Asians, I mean Korea, Japan, China, Vietnam, as distinct from Southeast Asia, which is a mix between the Sinic and the Indian, though Indian culture also emphasizes similar values."[7]

In fact, however, East Asia itself has much diversity, and there are many variations between Japan and China and Korea and other parts of East Asia. Various cultural influences from within and outside this region have affected human lives over the history of this rather large territory. These diverse influences still survive in a variety of ways. To illustrate, my copy of Houghton Mifflin's international *Almanac* describes the religions of the 124 million Japanese people in the following way: 112 million Shintoists and 93 million Buddhists. Buddhist practices coexist with Shinto practices, often within the same person's religious makeup. Cultures and traditions overlap over wide regions such as East Asia and even within specific countries such as Japan or China or Korea, and attempts at generalization about Asian values (with forceful—often brutal—implications for masses of people in this region with diverse faiths, convictions, and commitments) cannot but be extremely crude. Even the 2.8 million people of Singapore have vast variations in their cultural and historical traditions, despite the fact that the conformism surrounding Singapore's political leadership and the official interpretation of Asian values is very powerful at this time.

Freedom, Democracy, and Tolerance

The recognition of heterogeneity in Asian traditions does not, in any way, settle the issues of the presence or absence of a commitment to individual freedom and political liberty in Asian culture. It could be argued that the traditions extant in Asia differ

7. Fareed Zakaria, "Culture Is Destiny: A Conversation with Lee Kuan Yew," *Foreign Affairs* 73 (March/April 1994): 113.

among themselves, but nevertheless may share some common characteristics. It has been asserted, for example, that the treatment of elderly members of the family (such as aged parents) is more supportive in Asian countries than in the West. It is possible to argue about this claim, but there would be nothing very peculiar if similarities of this or other kinds were to obtain across the diverse culture of Asia: diversities need not apply to every field. The question that has to be asked, rather, is whether the Asian countries share the common feature of being skeptical of freedom and liberty, while emphasizing order and discipline. The advocates of Asian particularism often—explicitly or by implication—make this argument, which allows for heterogeneity within Asia, but asserts that there is a shared mistrust of the claims of liberal rights.

Authoritarian lines of reasoning often receive indirect backing from modes of thought in the West itself. There is clearly a tendency in the United States and Europe to assume, if only implicitly, the primacy of political freedom and democracy as a fundamental and ancient feature of Western culture—one not to be easily found in Asia. A contrast is drawn between the authoritarianism allegedly implicit in, say, Confucianism and the respect for individual liberty and autonomy allegedly deeply rooted in Western liberal culture. Western promoters of personal and political liberty in the non-Western world often see this as bringing Western values to Asia and Africa.

In all this, there is a substantial tendency to extrapolate backwards from the present. Values spread by the European Enlightenment and other relatively recent developments cannot be considered part of the long-term Western heritage, experienced in the West over millennia. Indeed, in answer to the question when and under what circumstances "the notion of individual liberty . . . first became explicit in the West," Isaiah Berlin has noted, "I have found no convincing evidence of any clear formulation of it in the ancient world."[8] This diagnosis has been disputed by Orlando Patterson, among others.[9] Patterson points to features in Western culture, particularly in Greece and Rome and in the tradition of Christianity, that indicate the presence of selective championing of individual liberty. The question that does not get adequately answered—indeed, it is scarcely even asked—is whether similar elements are absent in other cultures. Isaiah Berlin's thesis concerns the notion of individual freedom as we now understand it, and the absence of "any clear formulation" of this can coexist with the support and advocacy of *selected components* of the comprehensive notion that makes up the contemporary idea of individual liberty as an entitlement of everyone. Such components do exist in the Greco-Roman world and in the world of Christian thought, but we have to examine whether these components are present elsewhere as well—that is, in non-Western culture. We have to search for parts rather than the whole—both in the West and in Asia and elsewhere.

To illustrate this point, consider the idea that personal freedom for all is important for a good society. This claim can be seen as being composed of two distinct components, to wit, (1) *the value of personal freedom:* that personal freedom is important and should be guaranteed for those who "matter" in a good society, and (2) *equality of freedom:* that everyone matters and should have similar freedom. The two together entail that personal freedom should be guaranteed, on a shared basis, for all. Aristotle wrote much in the support of the former proposition, but in his exclusion of women and slaves did little to defend the latter. Indeed, the championing of equality in this form is of quite

8. Isaiah Berlin, *Four Essays on Liberty* (Oxford: Oxford University Press, 1969), xl.

9. See Orlando Patterson, *Freedom*, Vol. I: *Freedom in the Making of Western Culture* (New York: Basic Books, 1991).

recent origin. Even in a society stratified according to class and caste—such as the Mandarins and the Brahmins—freedom could be valued for the privileged, in much the same way freedom is valued for non-slave men in corresponding Greek conceptions of a good society.

Another useful distinction is between (1) *the value of toleration:* there must be toleration of diverse beliefs, commitments, and actions of different people, and (2) *equality of tolerance:* the toleration that is offered to some must be reasonably offered to all (except when tolerance of some will lead to intolerance for others). Again, arguments for some tolerance can be seen plentifully in earlier writings, without that tolerance being supplemented by equality of tolerance. The roots of modern democratic and liberal ideas can be sought in terms of constitutive elements, rather than as a whole.

Order and Confucianism

As part of this analytical scrutiny, the question has to be asked whether these constitutive components can be seen in Asian writings in the way they can be found in Western thought. The presence of these components must not be confused with the absence of the opposite, namely ideas and doctrines that clearly *do not* emphasize freedom and tolerance. Championing of order and discipline can be found in Western classics as well as in Asian ones. Indeed, it is by no means clear to me that Confucius is more authoritarian in this respect than, say, Plato or St. Augustine. The real issue is not whether these non-freedom perspectives are *present* in Asian traditions, but whether the freedom-oriented perspectives are *absent* there.

This is where the diversity of Asian value systems becomes central, incorporating but transcending regional diversity. An obvious example is the role of Buddhism as a form of thought.

In Buddhist tradition, great importance is attached to freedom, and the part of the earlier Indian theorizing to which Buddhist thoughts relate has much room for volition and free choice. Nobility of conduct has to be achieved in freedom, and even the ideas of liberation (such as *moksha*) have this feature. The presence of these elements in Buddhist thought does not obliterate the importance for Asia of ordered discipline emphasized by Confucianism, but it would be a mistake to take Confucianism to be the only tradition in Asia—indeed even in China. Since so much of the contemporary authoritarian interpretation of Asian values concentrates on Confucianism, this diversity is particularly worth emphasizing.

Indeed, the reading of Confucianism that is now standard among authoritarian champions of Asian values does less than justice to the variety within Confucius's own teachings, to which Simon Leys has recently drawn attention.[10] Confucius did not recommend blind allegiance to the state. When Zilu asks him "how to serve a prince," Confucius replies, "Tell him the truth even if it offends him."[11] Those in charge of censorship in Singapore or Beijing would take a very different view. Confucius is not averse to practical caution and tact, but does not forgo the recommendation to oppose a bad government. "When the [good] way prevails in the state, speak bolding and act boldly. When the state has lost the way, act boldly and speak softly."[12]

Indeed, Confucius provides a clear pointer to the fact that the two pillars of the imagined edifice of Asian values, namely loyalty to family and obedience to the state, can be in severe conflict with each other. The governor of She told Confucius, "Among my people, there is a man of unbending integrity: when his fa-

---

10. Simon Leys, *The Analects of Confucius* (New York: Norton, 1997).
11. Ibid., 14.22, p. 70.
12. Ibid., 14.3, p. 66.

ther stole a sheep, he denounced him." To this Confucius replied, "Among my people, men of integrity do things differently: a father covers up for his son, a son covers up for his father, and there is integrity in what they do."[13]

Elias Canetti has pointed out that in understanding the teachings of Confucius, we have to examine not only what he says, but also what he does not say.[14] The subtlety involved in what is often called "the silence of Confucius" has certainly escaped the modern austere interpreters in their tendency to assume that what is not explicitly supported must be implicitly forbidden. It is not my contention that Confucius was a democrat, or a great champion of freedom and political dissent, but there is reason enough to question the monolithic authoritarian image of him that is presented by the contemporary advocates of Asian values.

Freedom and Tolerance

If we shift our attention from China to the Indian subcontinent, we are in no particular danger of running into hard-to-interpret silence; it is difficult to outdo the Indian traditions of speaking at length and arguing endlessly in explicit and elaborate terms. India not only has the largest religious literature in the world, it also has by far the largest volume of atheistic and materialistic writings among the ancient civilizations. There is just a lot of literature of all kinds. The Indian epic *Mahabharata*, which is often compared with the *Iliad* or the *Odyssey*, is in fact seven times as long as the *Iliad* and *Odyssey* put together. In a well-known Bengali poem written in the nineteenth century by the religious and social leader Ram Mohan Ray, the real horror

---

13. Ibid., 13.18, p. 63.
14. Elias Canetti, *The Conscience of Words* (New York: Seabury Press, 1979); see also Leys, *The Analects of Confucius*, xxx–xxxii.

of death is described thus: "Just imagine how terrible it will be on the day you die, / Others will go on speaking, but you will not be able to respond."

This fondness for arguing, and for discussing things at leisure and at length, is itself somewhat in tension with the quiet order and discipline championed in the alleged Asian values. But in addition, the content of what has been written indicates a variety of views on freedom, tolerance, and equality. In many ways, the most interesting articulation of the need for tolerance on an egalitarian basis can be found in the writings of Emperor Ashoka, who in the third century B.C. commanded a larger Indian empire than any other Indian king in history (including the Moghuls, and even the Raj, if we leave out the native states that the British let be). He turned his attention in a big way to public ethics and enlightened politics after being horrified by the carnage he saw in his own victorious battle against the king of Kalinga (now Orissa). Ashoka converted to Buddhism and helped to make it a world religion by sending emissaries abroad with the Buddhist message. He also covered the country with stone inscriptions describing forms of good life and the nature of good government.

The inscriptions give a special importance to tolerance of diversity. For example, the edict (now numbered XII) at Erragudi puts the issue thus:

A man must not do reverence to his own sect or disparage that of another man without reason. Depreciation should be for specific reason only, because the sects of other people all deserve reverence for one reason or another.

By thus acting, a man exalts his own sect, and at the same time does service to the sects of other people. By acting contrariwise, a man hurts his own sect, and does disservice to the sects of other people. For he who does reverence to his own sect while disparaging the sects of others wholly from attachment to his own, with intent to enhance the splendour of his own sect, in reality by such conduct inflicts the severest injury on his own sect.[15]

These edicts from the third century B.C. emphasize the importance of tolerance, both in public policy by the government and in the behavior of citizens to each other.

On the domain and coverage of tolerance, Ashoka was a universalist and demanded this for all, including those whom he described as "forest people," the tribal population living in pre-agricultural economic formations. Condemning his own conduct before his conversion, Ashoka notes that in the war in Kalinga, "men and animals numbering one hundred and fifty thousands were carried away (captive) from that kingdom." He goes on to state that the slaughter or the taking of prisoners "of even a hundredth or thousandth part of all those people who were slain or died or were carried away (captive) at that time in Kalinga is now considered very deplorable [by him]." Indeed, he proceeds to assert that now he believes that even if a person should wrong him, that offense would be forgiven "if it is possible to forgive it." He describes the object of his government as "non-injury, restraint, impartiality, and mild behavior" applied "to all creatures."[16]

Ashoka's championing of egalitarian and universal tolerance may appear un-Asian to some commentators, but his views are firmly rooted in lines of analysis already in vogue in intellectual circles in India in the three preceding centuries. It is interesting, however, to consider another author whose treatise on governance and political economy was also profoundly influential. I refer to Kautilya, the author of *Arthashastra*, which can be trans-

15. Translation in Vincent A. Smith, *Asoka* (Delhi: S. Chand, 1964), pp. 170–71.

16. *Asokan Studies*, pp. 34–35, edict XIII.

lated as the "economic science," though it is at least as much concerned with practical politics as with economics. Kautilya, a contemporary of Aristotle, lived in the fourth century B.C. and worked as a senior minister of Emperor Chandragupta Maurya, Emperor Ashoka's grandfather, who had established the large Maurya empire across the subcontinent.

Kautilya's writing are often cited as a proof that freedom and tolerance were not valued in the Indian classical tradition. Two aspects of the impressively detailed account of economics and politics to be found in *Arthashastra* might tend to suggest that there is no support there for a liberal democracy.

First, Kautilya is a consequentialist of quite a narrow kind. While the objectives of promoting the happiness of subjects and order in the kingdom are strongly backed up by detailed policy advice, he depicts the king as a benevolent autocrat, whose power is to be maximized through good organization. Thus, *Arthashastra* presents penetrating ideas and suggestions on such practical subjects as famine prevention and administrative effectiveness that remain relevant even today, more than two thousand years later; yet at the same time, it advises the king how to get his way, if necessary though the violation of freedom of his opponents and adversaries.

Second, Kautilya seems to attach little importance to political or economic equality, and his vision of good society is strongly stratified according to lines of class and caste. Even though the objective of promoting happiness, which is given an exalted position in the hierarchy of values, is applied to all, the other objectives have clearly inegalitarian form and content. There is an obligation to give the less fortunate members of the society the support that they need to escape misery and enjoy life—Kautilya specifically identifies as the duty of the king to "provide the orphans, the aged, the infirm, the afflicted, and the helpless with maintenance," along with providing "subsistence to helpless women when they are carrying and also the [newborn] children they give birth to."[17] But recognizing that obligation is very far from valuing the freedom of these people to decide how to live—tolerating heterodoxy. Indeed, there is very little tolerance in Kautilya, expect for the upper sections of the community.

What do we conclude from this? Certainly, Kautilya is no democrat, no egalitarian, no general promoter of everyone's freedom. And yet, when it comes to the characterization of what the most favored people—the upper class—should get, freedom figures quite prominently. Denial of personal liberty of the upper classes (the so-called Arya) is seen as unacceptable. Indeed, regular penalties, some of them heavy, are specified for the taking of such adults or children in indenture, even though the slavery of the existing slaves is seen as perfectly acceptable.[18] To be sure, we do not find in Kautilya anything like the clear articulation that Aristotle provides of the importance of free exercise of capability. But the importance of freedom is clear enough in Kautilya as far as the upper classes are concerned. It contrasts with the governmental duties to the lower orders, which take the paternalistic form of state assistance for the avoidance of acute deprivation and misery. Still, insofar as a view of the good life emerges from all this, it is an ideal that is entirely consistent with a freedom-valuing ethical system. The domain of that concern is narrow, to be sure, confined to the upper groups of society, but this limitation is not wildly different from the Greek concern with free men as opposed to slaves or women.

I have been discussing in some detail the political ideas and practical reason presented by two forceful, but very different,

17. *Kautilya's Arthashastra*, translated by R. Shama Sastry (Mysore: Mysore Printing and Publishing House, 8th edition, 1967), p. 47.
18. See R. P. Kangle, *The Kautilya Arthashastra*, Part II (Bombay: University of Bombay, 1972), chapter 13, section 65, pp. 235–39.

expositors in India in the third and fourth centuries B.C. because their ideas have influenced later Indian writings. I do not want to give the impression that all Indian political commentators look lines of approach similar to Ashoka's or Kautilya's. Quite the contrary. Many positions taken before and after Kautilya and Ashoka contradict their respective claims, just as others are more in line either with Ashoka or with Kautilya.

For example, the importance of tolerance—even the need for universality in this—is eloquently expressed in different media, such as Shudraka's drama, Akbar's political pronouncements, and Kabir's poetry, to name just a few examples. The presence of these contributions does not entail the absence of opposite arguments and recommendations. Rather, the point is that in their heterogeneity, Indian traditions contain a variety of views and reasonings, but they include, in different ways, arguments in favor of tolerance, in defense of freedom, and even, in the case of Ashoka, in support of equality at a very basic level.

Akbar and Moghuls

Among the powerful expositors and practitioners of tolerance of diversity in India must be counted the great Moghul emperor Akbar, who reigned between 1556 and 1605. Again, we are not dealing with a democrat, but with a powerful king who emphasized the acceptability of diverse forms of social and religious behavior, and who accepted human rights of various kinds, including freedom of worship and religious practice. Such rights would not have been easily tolerated in parts of Europe in Akbar's time.

For example, as the year 1000 in the Muslim Hejira calendar was reached in 1591–92, there was excitement about it in Delhi and Agra (not unlike what is happening right now as the year 2000 in the Christian calendar approaches). Akbar issued various enactments at this juncture of history, and some of these focused on religious tolerance, including the following:

> No man should be interfered with on account of religion, and anyone [is] to be allowed to go over to a religion he pleased.
>   If a Hindu, when a child or otherwise, had been made a Muslim against his will, he is to be allowed, if he pleased, to go back to the religion of his fathers.[19]

Again, the domain of tolerance, while religion-neutral, was not universal in other respects, including gender equality or equality between younger and older people. The enactment went on to argue for the forcible repatriation of a young Hindu woman to her father's family if she had abandoned it in pursuit of a Muslim lover. In the choice between supporting the young lovers and the young woman's Hindu father, old Akbar's sympathies are entirely with the father. Tolerance and equality at one level are combined with intolerance and inequality at another level, but the extent of general tolerance on matters of belief and practice is quite remarkable. It is interesting to note, especially in light of the hard sell of "Western liberalism," that while Akbar was making these pronouncements on religious tolerance, the Inquisition was in high gear in Europe.

Theories and Practice

It is important to recognize that many of these historical leaders in Asia not only emphasized the importance of freedom and tolerance, they also had clear theories as to why this was the appropriate thing to do. This applies very strongly to both Ashoka and Akbar. Since the Islamic tradition is sometimes seen as

19. Translation from Vincent A. Smith, *Akbar: The Great Mogul* (Oxford: Clarendon Press, 1917), p. 257.

being monolithic, this is particularly important to emphasize in the case of Akbar. Akbar was, in fact, deeply interested in Hindu philosophy and culture, but also took much note of the beliefs and practices of other religions, including Christianity, Jainism, and the Parsee faith. In fact, he attempted to establish something of a synthetic religion for India—the Din Ilahi—drawing on the different faiths in the country.

There is an interesting contrast here between Ashoka's and Akbar's forms of religious tolerance. Both stood for religious tolerance by the state, and both argued for tolerance as a virtue to be practiced by all, but while Ashoka combined this with his own Buddhist pursuits (and tried to spread "enlightenment" at home and abroad), Akbar tried to combine the distinct religions of India, incorporating the "good points" of different religions. Akbar's court was filled with Hindu as well as Muslim intellectuals, artists, and musicians, and he tried in every way to be nonsectarian and symmetric in the treatment of his subjects.

It is also important to note that Akbar was by no means unique among the Moghul emperors in being tolerant. In many ways, the later Moghul emperor, the intolerant Aurangzeb, who violated many of what would be now seen as basic human rights of Hindus, was something of an exception.[20] But even Aurangzeb

20. The exponents of contemporary Hindu politics in India often try to deny the tolerant nature of much of Moghul rule. That tolerance was, however, handsomely acknowledged by Hindu leaders of an earlier vintage. For example, Sri Aurobindo, who established the famous ashram in Pondicherry, specifically identified this aspect of the Moghul rule (*The Spirit and Form of Indian Polity*, Calcutta: Arya Publishing House, 1947, pp. 86–89):

The Mussulman domination ceased very rapidly to be a foreign rule. . . . The Mogul empire was a great and magnificent construction and an immense amount of political genius and talent was employed in its creation and maintenance. It was as splendid, powerful and beneficent and, it may be added, in spite of Aurangzeb's fanatical zeal, infinitely more liberal and tolerant in religion than any medieval or contemporary European kingdom or empire.

should be considered in his familial setting, not in isolation. None of his immediate family seems to have shared Aurangzeb's intolerance. Dara Shikoh, his elder brother, was much involved with Hindu philosophy and had, with the help of some scholars, prepared a Persian translation of some of the *Upanishads*, the ancient texts dating from about the eighth century B.C. In fact, Dara Shikoh had much stronger claims to the Moghul throne than Aurangzeb, since he was the eldest and the favorite son of their father, Emperor Shah Jahan. Aurangzeb fought and killed Dara, and imprisoned their father for the rest of his life (leaving him, the builder of the Taj Mahal, to gaze at this creation in captivity, from a distance).

Aurangzeb's son, also called Akbar, rebelled against his father in 1681 and joined hands in this enterprise with the Hindu kingdoms in Rajasthan and later the Marathas (though Akbar's rebellion too was ultimately crushed by Aurangzeb). While fighting from Rajasthan, Akbar wrote to his father protesting his intolerance and vilification of his Hindu friends. The issue of tolerance of differences was indeed a subject of considerable discussion among the feuding parties. The father of the Maratha king, Raja Sambhaji, whom the young Akbar had joined, was no other than Shivaji, whom the present-day Hindu political activists treat as a superhero, and after whom the intolerant Hindu party Shiv Sena is named.

Shivaji himself took quite a tolerant view of religions differences. As the Moghul historian Khafi Kahn, who was no admirer of Shivaji in other respects, reports:

> [Shivaji] made it a rule that wherever his followers were plundering, they should do no harm to the mosques, the book of God, or the women of any one. Whenever a copy of the sacred

Quran came into his hands, he treated it with respect, and gave it to some of his Mussalman followers.[21]

In fact, a very interesting letter to Aurangzeb on the subject of tolerance is attributed to Shivaji by some historians (such as Sir Jadunath Sarkar, the author of the classic *Shivaji and His Times*, published in 1919), though there are some doubts about this attribution (another possible author is Rana Raj Singh of Mewar/Udaipur). No matter who among Aurangzeb's contemporaries wrote this letter, the ideas engaged in it are interesting enough. The letter contrasts Aurangzeb's intolerance with the tolerant policies of earlier Moghuls (Akbar, Jahangir, Shah Jahan), and then says this:

> If your Majesty places any faith in those books by distinction called divine, you will there be instructed that God is the God of all mankind, not the God of Muslims alone. The Pagan and the Muslim are equally in His presence. . . . In fine, the tribute you demand from Hindus is repugnant to justice.[22]

The subject of tolerance was indeed much discussed by many writers during this period of confrontation of religious traditions and the associated politics. One of the earliest writers on the subject of tolerance was the eleventh-century Iranian Alberuni, who came to India with the invading army of Sultan Mahmood of Ghazni and recorded his revulsion at the atrocities committed by the invaders. He proceeded to study Indian society, culture, religion, and intellectual pursuits (indeed his translations of Indian mathematical and astronomical treatises were quite influ-

21. *The Oxford History of India*, 4th edition, translated by Vincent Smith, edited by Percival Spear (London: Oxford University Press, 1974), p. 412.
22. Ibid., pp. 417–18.

ential in the Arab world, which in turn deeply influenced Western mathematics), but he also discussed the subject of intolerance
of the unfamiliar.

> In all manners and usages, [the Hindus] differ from us to such
> a degree as to frighten their children with us, with our dress,
> and our ways and customs, and as to declare us to be the devil's
> breed, and our doings as the very opposite of all that is good
> and proper. By the bye, we must confess, in order to be just, that
> a similar deprecation of foreigners not only prevails among us
> and the Hindus, but is common to all nation towards each
> other.[23]

The point of discussing all this is to indicate the presence of
conscious theorizing about tolerance and freedom in substantial
and important parts of Asian tradition. We could consider many
more illustrations of this phenomenon in writings from early
Arabic, Chinese, Indian, and other cultures. As was argued earlier, the championing of democracy and political freedom in the
modern sense cannot be found in the pre-Enlightenment tradition in any part of the world—the West or the East—so we have
to look at the constituent components of this compound idea.
The view that the basic ideas underlying freedom and rights in
tolerance society are "Western" notions, and somehow alien to
Asia, is hard to make any sense of, even though that view has
been championed by both Asian authoritarians and Western
chauvinists.

Intervention Across National Boundaries

I want to turn now to a rather different issue, which is sometimes linked to the debate about the nature and reach of Asian

23. *Alberuni's India*, translated by Edward C. Sachau, edited by Ainslie T.
Embree (New York: Norton, 1971), Part I, Chapter I, p. 20.

values. The championing of Asian values is often associated with the need to resist Western hegemony. The linking of the two issues, which has occurred increasingly in recent years, uses the political force of anticolonialism to buttress the assault on basic political and civil rights in postcolonial Asia.

This linkage, though quite artificial, can be rhetorically very effective. For example, Lee Kuan Yew has emphasized the special nature of Asian values and has made powerful use of the general case for resisting Western hegemony to bolster the argument for Asian particularism. The rhetoric has extended to the apparently defiant declaration that Singapore is "not a client state of America."[24] That fact is certainly undeniable, and is an excellent reason for cheer, but the question that has to be asked is what the bearing of this fact is on the issue of human rights and political liberties in Singapore or any other country in Asia.

The people whose political and other rights are involved in this debate are not citizens of the West, but of Asian countries. The fact that individual liberty and freedom may have been championed in Western writings and even by some Western political leaders can scarcely compromise the claim to liberty and freedom that people in Asia may otherwise have. As a matter of fact, one can grumble, with reason, that the political leaders of Western countries take far too *little* interest in issues of freedom in the rest of the world. There is plenty of evidence that the Western governments have, by and large, tended to give priority to the interests of their own citizens engaged in commerce with the Asian countries and to the pressures generated by business groups to be on good terms with the ruling governments in Asia. It is not so much that there has been more bark than bite; there has in fact been very little barking either. What Chairman Mao

24. *International Herald Tribune*, June 13, 1995, p. 4.

had once described as a "paper tiger" has increasingly looked like a paper mouse.

But even if this had not been the case, and even if Western governments really had tried to promote political and civil rights in Asia, how could that possibly compromise the status of the rights of Asians? In this context, the idea of "human rights" has to be properly spelled out. In the most general form, the notion of human rights builds on our shared humanity. These rights are not derived from the citizenship of any country, or the membership of any nation, but taken as entitlements of every human being. They differ, thus, from constitutionally created rights guaranteed for specified people (such as, say, American or French citizens). For example, the human right of a person not to be tortured is independent of the country of which this person is a citizen and thus exists irrespective of what the government of that country—or any other—wants to do. A government can, or course, dispute a person's *legal* right not to be tortured, but that will not amount to disputing what must be seen as the person's *human* right not to be tortured.

Since the conception of human rights transcends local legislation and the citizenship of the person affected, it is not surprising that support for human rights can also come from anyone—whether or not she is a citizen of the same country as the person whose rights are threatened. A foreigner does not need the permission of a repressive government to try to help a person whose liberties are being violated. Indeed, in so far as human rights are seen as rights that any person has as a human being and not as a citizen of any particular country, the reach of the corresponding *duties* can also include any human being, irrespective of citizenship.

This basic recognition does not, of course, suggest that everyone must intervene constantly in protecting and helping others. That may be both ineffective and unsettling. There is no escape from the need to employ practical reason in this field, any more than in any other field of deliberate human action. I have discussed elsewhere the nature of the necessary scrutiny, including the assessment of rights and their consequences.[25]

Ubiquitous interventionism is not particularly fruitful or attractive within a given country, or across national boundaries. There is no obligation to roam the four corners of the earth in search of liberties to protect. The claim is only that the barriers of nationality and citizenship do not preclude people from assuming some duties related to them. The moral and political examination that is central to determining how one should act applies across national boundaries and not merely within each realm.

A Concluding Remark

The so-called Asian values that are invoked to justify authoritarianism are not especially Asian in any significant sense. Nor is it easy to see how they could be made into an Asian cause against the West, by the mere force of rhetoric. The people whose rights are being disputed are Asians, and no matter what the West's guilt may be (there are many skeletons in many cupboards across the world), the rights of the Asians can scarcely be compromised on those grounds. The case for liberty and political rights turns ultimately on their basic importance and on their instrumental role. This case is as strong in Asia as it is elsewhere.

I have disputed the usefulness of a grand contrast between Asian and European values. There is a lot we can learn from studies of values in Asia and Europe, but they do not support or

---

25. Amartya Sen, "Rights and Agency," *Philosophy and Public Affairs* 11 (1982); "Liberty and Social Choice," *Journal of Philosophy* 80 (January 1983); "Well-Being, Agency and Freedom: The Dewey Lectures 1984," *Journal of Philosophy* 82 (April 1985).

sustain the thesis of grand dichotomy. Contemporary ideas of political and personal liberty and rights have taken their present form relatively recently, and it is hard to see them as "traditional" commitments of Western cultures. There are important antecedents of those commitments in the form of the advocacy of tolerance and individual freedom, but those antecedents can be found plentifully in Asian as well as Western cultures.

The recognition of diversity within different cultures is extremely important in the contemporary world, since we are constantly bombarded by oversimple generalizations about "Western civilization," "Asian values," "African cultures," and so on. These unfounded readings of history and civilization are not only intellectually shallow, they also add to the divisiveness of the world in which we live.

Authoritarian readings of Asian values that are increasingly being championed in some quarters do not survive scrutiny. The thesis of a grand dichotomy between Asian values and European values add little to our comprehension, and much to the confusion about the normative basis of freedom and democracy.

Minimal Ethical and Legal Absolutes in Foreign Trade

Foreign trade is an area about which much has been written. The majority of economists, going back to Adam Smith (1776), have generally concluded that trade is good and that it should be free and unhampered, at least most of the time. The reasoning behind their conclusion is almost always utilitarian based. Free and unrestricted trade is good because the majority benefits or because the gains from trade exceed the losses. In economic terms, one would say that trade is a positive-sum game. Economists—or, more likely, politicians—who say that trade should be restricted generally try to make a case for some special interest that has come to the legislature seeking protection.

The approach in this chapter is distinctively different from what one would find in a standard economics textbook. Although utilitarian approaches will be used to illustrate various points, the flaws inherent in any utilitarian approach are many. In fact, utilitarian arguments will be shown to be fatally flawed. Thus ethical arguments based on utilitarian approaches will be shown to be inferior to a rights approach. I show that trade protectionism, in any form, must necessarily violate individual rights. I also attempt to fill a gap in the trade literature that, until now, has almost always failed to view trade from the perspective of individual rights.

The Utilitarian Approach to Trade Policy

Whereas the utilitarian approach to trade policy is, as we shall see, fatally flawed, such an approach often leads to the same conclusion that a rights approach would reach, only for the wrong reason. Before we criticize the utilitarian approach, let us spend a few minutes reviewing how the utilitarian approach is commonly applied to trade policy. We will then be better able to contrast the utilitarian approach with the rights approach.

Efficiency

The main economic argument for unrestricted trade is efficiency. It is easier to buy oranges and bananas if you live in Maine than to grow them yourself. David Ricardo's Law of Comparative Advantage (1817) points out that everyone is better off if they specialize in what they do best and trade for everything else. (Adam Smith said the same thing in 1776.) Productivity is enhanced by producing only the things you are best at producing and allowing others to do the same. Everyone can have more of everything if they concentrate their efforts on what they do best and trade for everything else.

The key to maximizing a society's total wealth is free trade. It makes no sense to specialize in what you do best if you are not able to trade what you have for what you want. So a necessary corollary of specialization is the ability to trade freely. That is why economists generally conclude that free trade is the best policy.

Tariffs and Quotas: The Standard Tools of Protectionists

If economists generally agree that free trade is the best policy, why is it that practically no country on earth, including the United States, has free trade? A simple, if incomplete, answer is that economists are not in charge of trade policy, politicians are.

Although most economists can see the benefits of free trade, politicians generally cannot. One reason for their blindness is their constituencies. Special interests constantly bombard politicians with requests for protection from foreign (or even domestic) competition. Consumers seldom, if ever, provide a countervailing argument for free trade. Political systems have a structural bias in favor of special interests and against the general public.

Let's take shirts for example. The average shirt in the United States costs $5 more than it would if there were no tariffs or quotas (Hufbauer et al. 1986) because the U.S. Congress has seen fit to pass legislation that places tariffs or quotas or both on the importation of foreign textiles and apparel. This cost of protectionism will not change in the near future even though the creation of the World Trade Organization and its many thousands of pages of rules and regulations are supposedly aimed at reducing or eliminating tariffs and quotas at some point in the future. The average consumer doesn't know that his representatives in Congress are costing him an extra $5 each time he buys a shirt; even if he did know, the cost of going to Washington to protest would be far more, in terms of out-of-pocket costs and time lost, than is the cost of the few shirts he buys each year.

Domestic textile and apparel manufacturers have a great deal at stake in trade policy, so it is worth their time and effort to go to the legislature to lobby for laws that will benefit them, even if it is at the expense of the general public. Public choice economists call this activity rent seeking (Buchanan, Tollison, and Tullock 1980). This kind of activity exists whenever the benefits of a policy are concentrated and the costs are disbursed or spread among a significant portion of the general public. Vilfredo Pareto summed it up in 1927 when he said:

> Even if it were very clearly demonstrated that protection always entails the destruction of wealth, if that were taught to every

citizen just as they learn the abc's, protection would lose so small a number of partisans and free trade would gain so few of them that the effect can be almost, or even completely, disregarded. The motives which lead men to act are quite different.

In order to explain how those who champion protection make themselves heard so easily, it is necessary to add a consideration which applies to social movements generally. The intensity of the work of an individual is not proportionate to the benefits which that work may bring him nor to the harm which it may enable him to avoid. If a certain measure A is the case of the loss of one franc to each of a thousand persons, and of a thousand franc gain to one individual, the latter will expend a great deal of energy, whereas the former will resist weakly; and it is likely that, in the end, the person who is attempting to secure the thousand francs via A will be successful.

A protectionist measure provides large benefits to a small number of people, and causes a very great number of consumers a slight loss. This circumstance makes it easier to put a protectionist measure into practice. (Pareto 1927, 377, 379.)

Tariffs and quotas have traditionally been the tools of preference for protectionists. Although the techniques are different, the effect is the same. Quotas and tariffs both protect some special interest at the expense of the general public. Thus, they both fail the utilitarian test because the majority is harmed. Nearly every study that has ever been made has concluded that the cost of protecting a particular item exceeds the benefits to be received.

The net deadweight loss can be computed in several ways. It can be computed in monetary units to show how much, in terms of dollars, yen, or another currency, some protectionist measure costs consumers. It can also be measured in terms of percentages to show that a certain protectionist measure causes the price of some selected product to increase by 30 percent or whatever.

A Brookings Institution study found that a particular voluntary restraint agreement on the importation of foreign cars cost consumers about $14 billion in 1984 and allowed domestic auto profits to increase by $9 billion, for a deadweight loss of $5 billion (Clifford 1987). A study of a pre-1985 steel agreement with the European Community estimated that the induced increase in the price of foreign steel was 30 percent and that the restraint on foreign producers also allowed the domestic steel industry to increase its prices by 12 percent (Hufbauer et al. 1986). A study of the textile industry estimated that protectionist measures caused the price of domestic textiles to increase by 21 percent (Hufbauer et al. 1986, 146). Another textile study estimated the domestic price increase to be 28 percent (Cline 1990). Various studies of the apparel industry have estimated that protectionist measures add 39 percent, 50 percent, 46 percent, 76 percent, or 53 percent to the cost of apparel items (McGee 1994b, 67). The various farm commodity programs had an annual deadweight loss of $6 billion in 1987, according to one estimate (Gardner 1990).

Deadweight losses can also be measured by the cost of every job saved or the net number of jobs that are destroyed by some protectionist policy. One study found that a particular protectionist policy would save thirty-six thousand apparel manufacturing jobs but would destroy fifty-eight thousand jobs in the retailing end of the apparel industry, for a loss/gain ratio of more than 1.6 to 1.0 (Baughman and Emrich 1987). A study of voluntary restraints in the steel industry estimated that the agreement saved 16,900 jobs in the steel industry but destroyed 52,400 jobs in the industries that use steel, for a loss/gain ratio of 3.1 to 1.0 (Denzau 1987). Various studies have estimated that the cost to consumers for each job saved in the benzenoid chemical industry to be more than $1 million; $200,000 in glassware; $30,000 in rubber footwear; $135,000 in ceramic tiles; $240,000 in orange juice; $76,000 in canned tuna; $750,000 in carbon steel; and $1 million in specialty steel (McGee 1994b, 79).

Antidumping Laws

Antidumping laws, while less visible to the average consumer, may become the protectionist tool of choice since the conclusion of the Uruguay Round and the creation of the World Trade Organization supposedly will result in the reduction or elimination of tariffs and quotas sometime in the distant future. Briefly stated, antidumping laws protect consumers from low prices. Of course, what antidumping laws actually do is protect domestic producers from foreign competition.

Here is how it works. If a domestic producer feels threatened by a foreign competitor, all it has to do is complain to Washington (or London, Rome, or whatever) that the foreign producer is dumping its product on the market. According to the antidumping laws in most countries, and according to the antidumping provisions that are part of the World Trade Organization (WTO), the foreign producer will be found guilty of dumping if it either sells its product on some domestic market for a lower price than the price it charges in its home market or if it sells for less than the cost of production, whatever that means. Actually, the way the cost of production is computed under U.S. law, it is possible for a foreign producer to be found guilty of dumping even if it sells its product in the United States for 7 percent more than the cost of production. It is also possible under U.S. rules to be found guilty of dumping even if the foreign producer sells the same product for the same identical price worldwide (Knoll 1987, 278; McGee 1993).

If a foreign producer is found guilty of dumping, there are several possible remedies. It can either be forced to raise its prices, or it can be prevented from selling its products in the domestic market for a certain number of years. Either way, consumers lose and domestic producers gain.

The administration of the antidumping laws in the United

States is truly bizarre, and the administration in other countries is not always that much different, since many countries have modeled their antidumping laws after those of the United States. The antidumping laws are among the most unjust of any laws on the books in the United States. David Palmeter sums up the injustice as follows:

> Imagine a system of civil litigation in which a party serves a massive discovery request, consisting of interrogatories and requests for production of documents. Imagine further that the serving party has the sole authority to prescribe the time within which response must be made and the format (such as to require multiple copies and translation into English of all requested documents originally prepared in a foreign language). Imagine still further that the serving party is the sole judge of the response and of the merits of all objections as to relevance or burdensomeness of the request; that the serving party also is the imposer of sanctions for failure to comply, and the ultimate decision-maker in the underlying matter for which the information is sought.
>
> Such a system would be intolerable in the state or federal courts of the United States. It would raise serious questions of due process in a system of administrative law that separates the investigative from the judicial function within a single agency. But this is the inquisitorial system that was ordained by Congress for the administration of the antidumping and countervailing duty provisions of Title VII of the Tariff Act of 1930. Torquemada, no doubt, would be right at home with it. But this is hardly a recommendation for the system. It should be changed. (Palmeter 1986, 641)

The antidumping laws invite abuse. Indeed, they have become among the most abused laws on the books. Subject to certain minor restraints, all a domestic producer need do is complain to the Commerce Department that some foreign competitor is dumping and the Commerce Department will take it from there. The foreign producer will have to spend perhaps millions of dollars defending itself in various administrative courts. The odds are stacked against winning because of the way the cost of production is defined. Also, if the accused foreigner is not able to produce 100 percent of the data the Commerce Department wants, when it wants it, and in the form it demands, the Commerce Department is free to totally ignore all the evidence the foreigner has submitted and use unreliable estimates that the domestic producer has submitted instead. It is an abuse of the legal system that such a procedure exists. Yet, because antidumping laws have been incorporated into the WTO, it is likely that such abuses will not only continue but become more widespread.

One of the more outrageous examples of Commerce Department abuse involved Matsushita, which withdrew from an antidumping case that involved small-business telephone systems. Matsushita's withdrawal caused it to abandon more than $50 million in annual export sales because of impossible demands by the Commerce Department to produce evidence. On a Friday afternoon, the Commerce Department demanded that Matsushita translate three thousand pages of Japanese financial documents into English by the following Monday morning (Bovard 1991, 136).

One weakness of the utilitarian approach to economics is its failure to consider questions of basic fairness. Utilitarianism seldom, if ever, goes beyond discussions of deadweight gains and losses. Interestingly enough, a study by the U.S. International Trade Commission, which jointly administers the antidumping laws with the Commerce Department, published a study (1995) that provides empirical evidence that the antidumping laws result in deadweight losses. This study, which estimated the gains and losses for only a fraction of the antidumping and countervailing duty orders that were outstanding in 1991, found that the net deadweight loss involving just the directly affected parties was $1.85 billion. The gains to the rest of the economy that would have occurred if the antidumping and countervailing duty orders then in force were removed were estimated to be between $2.17 billion and $2.94 billion.

Trade Sanctions, Embargoes, and Blockades

Trade sanctions, embargoes, and blockades fail the efficiency test for utilitarians because implementing them reduces efficiency and wealth. Yet these practices exist and are even widespread. How can that be, especially if there are no special interests pushing for government to protect them by using one of these tools? The theory is that some things are more important than efficiency or wealth creation. We do not trade with evil regimes, we do not buy products that are made with slave labor or child labor, we do not wear makeup that includes animal testing as part of the manufacturing or research and development process, we do not eat tuna that is sold by companies whose nets also harvest dolphins, we do not allow our citizens to trade with countries that are at war with an ally, and so on. Trade sanctions, embargoes, and blockades thus do not lend themselves to utilitarian analysis, so we will defer discussion of them until later.

What's Wrong with Utilitarianism?

Utilitarian approaches generally lead to the conclusion that free trade is the best policy because the results are generally beneficial. Gains from trade exceed losses. Free trade results in lower prices or a wider selection of goods or both. If free trade destroys jobs, it also creates more jobs than it destroys.

Although utilitarian approaches usually lead to the correct conclusion—that free trade is good and beneficial—they do so for the wrong reason. At its core, the utilitarian philosophy is rabidly majoritarian. Utilitarians would conclude that free trade is good because the majority benefits. A rights approach yields the same conclusion—that free trade is good—but for an entirely different reason. For a rights theorist, free trade is good because it is the only trade regime that does not violate rights (McGee 1994a).

One major problem with any utilitarian analysis is that it does not provide a way to measure gains and losses (Rothbard 1970, 260–68). Gains and losses may only be estimated. The numerous studies that *have* attempted to measure the gains and losses of various trade or other policies are just that: attempts. Because there is no way of knowing precisely how many jobs are saved or lost as a result of a particular trade policy, assumptions and estimates have to be made. Likewise, because there are so many economic variables that interact with one another and no one knows precisely how they should fit into the equation, there is no way to know precisely how much more consumers must pay for a shirt as a result of some piece of trade legislation. Human action determines values and prices, and there is no way to input that data into a computer.

Another flaw inherent in any utilitarian analysis is that consumer choices are in terms of rank, not dollars or percentages. If a particular consumer prefers the hamburgers made at restaurant A rather than restaurant B, all one can say is that he prefers A's hamburgers to B's. One cannot say that A's hamburgers are 14.3 percent better than B's hamburgers or that a particular consumer prefers A's hamburgers to B's by 14.3 percent.

Another insoluble problem with any utilitarian analysis is that not all individuals stand to gain or lose the same amount as a result of this policy or that. Thus it is impossible to measure total gains and total losses when the amount of the gain or loss differs between and among individuals. For example, millions of consumers stand to lose a little if a piece of protectionist trade legislation is passed that causes the price of shirts to rise. But domestic manufacturers of shirts, as well as their down-line suppliers, stand to gain much if restrictive trade legislation is passed. How can one determine whether the few who stand to gain much benefit more than the many who lose just a little, especially if some of the people who work for the domestic producers wear shirts?

These workers will benefit because their jobs are protected, but they will lose because they must also pay more for the shirts they buy. Also, since the textile and apparel industries pay lower than average wages, some of the workers who would be displaced in the absence of protectionist trade legislation may be able to find higher-paying jobs in some other industry.

Not everyone who loses a job is worse off. Some people actually are better off, in terms of either dollars or intangibles. Some people who lose jobs find other jobs that pay more or have better working conditions. Is someone who loses a job but finds another job that pays 10 percent less but requires 20 percent fewer working hours worse off or better off, especially if he enjoys spending leisure time with the family? What if she lands a new job that pays 10 percent more but requires 20 percent more working hours? Is she better off? Utilitarians and number-crunching economists are unable to answer those questions.

There is no way to accurately measure the total gains and losses that result from a particular protectionist measure because it is impossible to predict where the money will flow in the absence of protectionism. But it can be concluded, a priori, that total satisfaction will decrease if consumers have to settle for their second or third choice because some protectionist measure prevents them from buying their first choice.

Inherent in the utilitarian approach is the underlying view that governments have some inherent right to regulate trade. The U.S. Constitution states that "the Congress shall have Power to regulate Commerce with foreign Nations"; however, having the authority is not the same as having the right. An extreme example of this distinction is Nazi Germany. Under the Hitler regime, soldiers had the authority to kill Gypsies, Jews, and Poles. But they did not have the right to do so. The same is true of trade. Governments have the authority to regulate trade, but they do not have the right. Any government action that prevents consenting adults from entering into contracts and trading the property they have for the property they want goes beyond the legitimate functions of government. That some constitution grants government the authority does not change this basic fact.

There is a grain of truth to the argument that "the people" have consented to this trade restriction. When the U.S. Constitution was written, some representatives of the people went to Philadelphia to hammer out a set of rules for a new nation. The final product was the U.S. Constitution. It could in no way be said, however, that this Constitution drew the approval of 100 percent of the people. Indeed, some states refused to ratify it until a bill of rights was added. And even then there were many people who did not want to see it adopted (Spooner 1973).

A long-established rule of common law is that no one can make a contract that someone else may be bound to without that person's consent. Another long-established principle of common law is that no one may enter into a contract that binds people who are not yet born. Thus, the U.S. Constitution cannot bind anyone who was not born at the date of its signing.

We are all bound by it, in any case, because the government punishes us if we violate this supreme law of the land. The Constitution is, however, utilitarian based since some majority, at some time in the past, made rules that supposedly bind all of us. The problem is that some people may have their rights violated by certain terms in the Constitution, such as giving the government the power to regulate trade, when all trade should be between consenting adults and free from government restraints.

The Rights Approach

The rights approach is superior to the utilitarian approach because of the utilitarian approach's inability to measure gains and losses or interpersonal utility. Under the rights approach, which does not require us to make any such calculations, one may determine whether a policy is minimally ethical merely by determining whether anyone's rights have been violated. If rights have been violated, then the policy fails to pass the test of minimal ethical acceptability. If no one's rights are violated, then the policy passes the test.

The rights I am talking about here are negative rights, which must be distinguished from positive rights. Also, different levels of ethics must be distinguished. For example, if a specific trade policy does not result in the violation of anyone's negative rights, then such trade should not be prohibited because the minimal level of ethical conduct has been achieved. It would be unethical for some individual or group of individuals to prevent such exchanges from taking place. But it does not follow that the individuals who engage in all such trades are acting ethically. Take prostitution. Neither the prostitute nor the client violates anyone's rights, which means that it is unethical for anyone to prevent the transaction from taking place. But it does not follow that the prostitute or the client is acting ethically, for prostitution may be considered unethical by some people. The same argument could be made for drug dealers, pimps, sellers of pornography, coffee, red meat, ham and cheese sandwiches, and so on. Unethical acts should be prohibited only if they violate someone's negative rights.

NEGATIVE AND POSITIVE RIGHTS

Since it is my position that only acts that violate negative rights should be prohibited, I need to say a few words about the distinction between negative and positive rights, which is that negative rights can never conflict, whereas positive rights must necessarily conflict with negative rights. Another distinction is that negative rights are inherent, whereas positive rights are granted by governments.

Negative rights, then, are preexisting rights. They come before government. Indeed, one of the main reasons for the creation of governments is to protect negative rights. Negative rights include the rights to life, liberty, and property. Stated negatively, they are the rights not to have your life, liberty, or property taken from you without your consent. Positive rights, in contrast, are granted by governments to some individuals or groups at the expense of other individuals or groups. An example is rent control laws. If the market value of an apartment is $1,500 a month, and rent control prohibits the landlord from charging more than $800, the tenant's right to subsidized rent is at the landlord's expense. Thus the landlord's negative right to property is violated to the extent of $700 a month since that is the extra amount he would be able to charge in the absence of the rent control. Rent control thus effectively taxes the landlord $700 a month and transfers the $700 to the tenant.

Many laws are based on the theory of positive rights. Antidiscrimination laws, for example, prevent landlords, restaurant owners, and others from refusing to enter into contracts with the people of their choosing. Thus, a black person's right to eat anywhere he wants is gained only at the expense of any restaurant owners who would otherwise refuse service. Any law that awards rights to one person or group at the expense of some other person or group is illegitimate and goes beyond the proper scope of government.

Frederic Bastiat, the nineteenth-century French philosopher and economist, formulated the following rule for determining whether a particular law was legitimate:

> See if the law takes from some persons what belongs to them, and gives it to other persons to whom it does not belong. See if the law benefits one citizen at the expense of another by doing what the citizen himself cannot do without committing a crime. Then abolish this law without delay, for it is not only an evil itself, but also it is a fertile source for further evils because it invites reprisals. If such a law—which may be an isolated case— is not abolished immediately, it will spread, multiply, and develop into a system. (Bastiat 1968, 21)

In Bastiat's view, then, all laws establishing positive rights must be abolished because they necessarily result in the taking of property from some to give it to others who have not earned it. One can easily apply Bastiat's rule to trade policy. Tariffs, quotas, and antidumping laws are the result of some special interest going to the appropriate legislature and asking for protection. To purchase the foreign product, consumers must part with more of their money than would be the case under a free trade regime. The domestic producer, who has done nothing to earn the higher price, benefits. Protectionism necessarily violates individual rights (McGee and Block 1997b).

AN OVERLOOKED ETHICAL ISSUE

Now let's turn the tables a bit and take a perspective that has been almost totally absent from both the business and the ethics literature. Is it unethical for someone to go to the government and ask for protection, whether it be in the form of a tariff, quota, or antidumping action? W. M. Curtiss has an interesting reply:

> Through the years, some men have discovered how to satisfy their wants at the expense of others without being accused of theft: they ask their government to do the stealing for them. (Curtiss 1953, 19)

A well-established principle of agency law is that the principal is responsible for the acts of his agent. Thus, if John hires Jill to kill someone, both John and Jill are guilty of murder. John cannot escape liability for the crime by arguing that it was actually Jill who did the killing. Likewise, if an individual representing a special interest, let's say the steel industry, goes to Congress and asks for a higher tariff on the importation of foreign steel or a limitation on the amount of foreign steel that can enter the country, is it any different than if individuals or a group cause the price of foreign steel to go up or stop foreign steel shipments at the border? The effect is exactly the same. Consumers either have to pay higher prices or do without some product that some of them would otherwise buy.

Initiating an antidumping action also presents an interesting ethical question that has gone practically unasked in the literature (McGee and Block 1997a). Is it unethical for someone to initiate an antidumping action? The answer is yes, whether one takes a utilitarian or rights approach. Let's see why.

It is wrong to take property that does not belong to you. Likewise, it is wrong to destroy property that belongs to someone else. Initiating an antidumping action, in essence, amounts to stealing the property of consumers and destroying the property of foreign competitors. Let's start with the stealing analogy.

When individuals from a domestic producer go to the Commerce Department to launch an antidumping investigation, it is with the intent of either forcing the targeted foreign competitor out of the domestic market altogether or forcing it to raise its prices. Either way, consumers lose. If the foreign producer is forced out of the domestic market, some consumers will have to settle for a less desirable product because the government has prevented them from trading with the producer who would have been their first choice.

Because a major competitor has been forced from the market, there is less downward pressure on prices, meaning that domestic producers do not feel a need to keep their prices low because they do not have to face fierce foreign competition. Thus, consumers have the choice of either paying a higher price for a domestic product or doing without it. The difference between the price they would have paid in a competitive market and the price they now have to pay because of less foreign competition goes into the pocket of the domestic producer(s) who initiated the antidumping action. Those producers thus used the force of government to feather their nests at the expense of the general public, for if they receive an extra $20 a unit because of the antidumping action, the effect is exactly the same as if they stole $20 at gunpoint from every consumer who bought their product. The only difference is that it is the government's gun that was pointed at the head of the foreign producer rather than the head of the consumer. But since the government (Commerce Department) was acting as the agent of the domestic producers, in effect the theft was committed by the domestic producers. It makes no difference whether the agent or the principal does the stealing; either way the consumer is getting fleeced.

Antidumping laws also destroy the property of the targeted foreign producers. Once an antidumping investigation is launched, the targeted foreign producers have to expend large sums of money on expensive lawyers and accountants to defend themselves, sometimes amounting to a million dollars or more.

Whether or not they are found guilty, they still incur large expenses to defend themselves for something they have every right to do—sell their products to willing consumers at mutually agreed-on prices. Antidumping actions force targeted foreign producers to dissipate their assets in frivolous lawsuits to defend themselves, which has the same effect on the bottom line as setting fire to a million-dollar warehouse. Destruction by arson may be more visible, but the effect on the bottom line is exactly the same. Yet arson is a felony, whereas launching an antidumping investigation is perfectly legal.

One might make the predatory pricing argument to justify at least some antidumping actions, but on analysis this argument falls flat. First, predatory pricing doesn't exist. It is like a unicorn that exists on paper and in people's minds but does not exist in reality (Koller 1971). Second, if it did exist, it would benefit consumers since the result would be lower prices. If a competitor actually did succeed in driving all other competitors from the market by predatory pricing, it would have to keep prices low. Otherwise, new competitors would enter the market. Thus attempts to reap monopoly profits by resorting to predatory pricing would be futile.

It is true that, in the absence of antidumping laws, some domestic competitors would go out of business. Antidumping laws allow weak domestic competitors to stay in business since consumers are not free to vote with their dollars to buy the products of foreign producers that cannot enter the country or that can enter the country only at prohibitively high prices. It should be kept in mind, however, that going out of business because of market forces does not violate anyone's rights.

To use a simple analogy, let's say that a large supermarket opens up across the street from a mom-and-pop grocery store. The supermarket is open twenty-four hours a day and offers a wide selection of products at low prices. Mom and pop will almost surely be harmed by the competition and may even be driven out of business. But their rights have not been violated. They still have inventory; they still have the right to sell it to willing consumers. Mom and pop have no right to force unwilling consumers to pay higher prices for their products when the products are available across the street for lower prices.

The same is true of any other products made or sold in the domestic market. General Motors, Ford, and Chrysler have no right to force consumers to buy their products. Consumers have the right to vote with their dollars to purchase the products of foreign automakers. When that right is taken from them, whether because of antidumping laws, tariffs, or quotas, consumers have their rights violated by the individuals at the domestic auto companies who used the force of government to insulate their companies from foreign competition.

Embargoes, Sanctions, and Blockades

Trade embargoes, economic sanctions, and blockades do not pass the utilitarian test for morality because they are all negative-sum games. The losers always outnumber the winners because everyone is a loser. The targeted countries or producers lose sales. Consumers in the country that established the embargo, sanction, or blockade lose because they are unable to enter into buy and sell contracts with the targeted country. Yet these punitive actions, which are not only condoned but given the status of morally superior actions, constitute the rare occasions when utilitarian analysis is thrown out the window and replaced with decisionmaking that, on the surface at least, is based on nonutilitarian morality.

A closer analysis soon reveals, however, that embargoes, sanctions, and blockades are *immoral* because they violate the rights of consenting adults to enter into contracts and exchange the property they have for the property they want. Interestingly, the trade and ethics literature is almost completely silent on this point (McGee 1998).

To analyze the morality of embargoes, sanctions, and blockades, let us begin with the nonaggression axiom that initiation of force is never justified. Trade embargoes, economic sanctions, and blockades all involve force or the threat of force since the government punishes anyone who violates the embargo, sanction, or blockade. The fact that some blockades, sanctions, or embargoes may have been started for noble reasons does not alter the fact that all these actions violate the nonaggression axiom and are thus immoral on their face, regardless of why the embargo, sanction, or blockade was put in place.

Automatic violation of the nonaggression axiom, coupled with the fact that the vast majority of embargoes, sanctions, and blockades have been unsuccessful (Hufbauer et al. 1990), destroys the argument that these actions are morally justified. Indeed, there is never any moral justification for preventing consenting adults from entering into contracts as long as no one's negative rights are violated.

Strong arguments can be made to justify some sanctions or embargoes from an individualist perspective. There may be good reasons why individuals should not trade with the likes of Castro, Stalin, Mao, Israel, or whatever, but those decisions should be left to individuals, not governments, which have no moral authority to prevent trade between consenting adults in the first place. Individuals should make those decisions for themselves.

There is strong evidence to show that governmentally imposed restrictions on trade have resulted in wars. For instance, Roosevelt's blockade of raw materials against the Japanese in Manchuria during the 1930s arguably led to the bombing of Pearl Harbor (Willett and Jalalighajar 1983/84, 725; Martin 1977, 114). World War I was preceded by tariff and trade wars, and many other wars were, in part at least, the result of protectionist trade policies (Turner 1970; Taylor 1983). Perhaps the earliest recorded case of trade sanctions leading to war occurred in 432 B.C., when Athens imposed trade sanctions on Megara, triggering the Peloponnesian War (Bartlett 1985, 1).

Individual Rights:
The Minimal Legal and Ethical Absolute

Economists and most philosophers have used utilitarian-based theories to determine the dividing line between good and bad trade policy. But utilitarian approaches, as we have seen, have several fatal flaws. For one thing, there is no way to measure gains and losses, so one can never be sure whether the gains exceed the losses. A small minority might gain much while the vast majority lose little individually. The analysis thus tends to break down into untrammeled majoritarianism. But even the slide into majoritarianism will not solve the gain/loss question because it is not possible to precisely measure whether a small loss by a large majority can be offset by a large gain by a small special interest, resulting in a net positive benefit.

But an even worse flaw in the majoritarianism approach is the total disregard of individual rights. A utilitarian would approve a trade policy even if someone's rights were violated as long as total utility was deemed to be increased by adoption of the policy. When one breaks down trade policy to its essentials, however, one finds nothing more than individual contracts—individuals trading what they have for what they want. Thus trade policy is nothing more than an application of contract, property, and association rights. Governments were formed to protect these rights, and any government that disparages these rights loses its legitimacy. The measure of whether a trade policy meets minimum legal and ethical standards is whether it violates anyone's property, contract or association rights. If it does, then it fails to meet the minimal ethical standard.

Bibliography

Bartlett, Bruce. "What's Wrong with Trade Sanctions?" *Policy Analysis* (Cato Institute), no. 64 (1985).

Bastiat, Frederic. *The Law*. Irvington-on-Hudson, N.Y.: Foundation for Economic Education, 1968.

Baughman, Laura Megna, and Thomas Emrich. *Analysis of the Impact of the Textile and Apparel Trade Enforcement Act of 1985*. International Business and Economic Research Corporation, 1985. Cited in I. M. Destler and John S. Odell. *Anti-Protection: Changing Forces in United States Trade Politics*. Washington, D.C.: Institute for International Economics, 1987, pp. 54, 56.

Bovard, James. *The Fair Trade Fraud*. New York: St. Martin's Press, 1991.

Buchanan, James, Robert Tollison, and Gordon Tullock, eds. *Towards a Theory of the Rent Seeking Society*. College Station: Texas A&M University Press, 1980.

Clifford Winston and Associates. *Blind Intersection? Policy and the Automobile Industry*. Washington, D.C.: Brookings Institution, 1987. This study is summarized in Thomas D. Hopkins, *Cost of Regulation*. Rochester, N.Y.: Rochester Institute of Technology, 1991, pp. B8–9.

Cline, William R. *The Future of World Trade in Textiles and Apparel*. Washington, D.C.: Institute for International Economics, 1990.

Curtiss, W. M. *The Tariff Idea*. Irvington-on-Hudson, N.Y.: Foundation for Economic Education, 1953.

Denzau, Arthur T. *How Import Restraints Reduce Employment*. Saint Louis: Washington University, Center for the Study of American Business, 1987.

Gardner, Bruce L. "The United States." In Fred H. Sanderson, ed., *Agricultural Protectionism in the Industrialized World*. Washington, D.C.: Resources for the Future, 1990.

Hufbauer, Gary Clyde, Diane T. Berliner, and Kimberly Ann Elliott. *Trade Protection in the United States: 31 Case Studies*. Washington, D.C.: Institute for International Economics, 1986.

Hufbauer, Gary Clyde, Jeffrey J. Schott, and Kimberly Ann Elliott. *Eco-

nomic Sanctions Reconsidered: History and Current Policy. 2d ed. Washington, D.C.: Institute for International Economics, 1990.

———. *Economic Sanctions Reconsidered: Supplemental Case Histories.* 2d ed. Washington, D.C.: Institute for International Economics, 1990.

Knoll, M. S. "United States Antidumping Law: The Case for Reconsideration." *Texas International Law Journal* 22 (1987): 265–90.

Koller, R., Jr. "The Myth of Predatory Pricing: An Empirical Study." *Antitrust Law & Economics Review* 4 (1971): 105–23.

Martin, James J. "Pearl Harbor: Antecedents, Background and Consequences." In James J. Martin, *The Saga of Hog Island.* Colorado Springs, Colo.: Ralph Myles Publisher, 1977, pp. 114–31.

McGee, Robert W. "Trade Embargoes, Sanctions and Blockades: Some Overlooked Human Rights Issues." *Journal of World Trade* 32, no. 4 (August 1998): 139–44.

———. "The Case to Repeal the Antidumping Laws." *Northwestern Journal of International Law & Business* 13 (spring 1993): 491–562.

———. "The Fatal Flaw in NAFTA, GATT and All Other Trade Agreements." *Northwestern Journal of International Law & Business* 14 (spring 1994a): 549–65.

———. *A Trade Policy for Free Societies: The Case against Protectionism.* Westport, Conn.: Quorum Books, 1994b.

McGee, Robert W., and Walter Block. "Ethical Aspects of Initiating Antidumping Actions." *International Journal of Social Economics* 24 (1997a): 599–608.

———. "Must Protectionism Always Violate Rights?" *International Journal of Social Economics* 24 (1997b): 393–407.

Palmeter, N. David. "Torquemada and the Tariff Act: The Inquisitor Rides Again." *International Lawyer* 20 (1986): 641.

Pareto, Vilfredo. *Manual of Political Economy.* Various publishers, 1927.

Ricardo, David. *Principles of Political Economy and Taxation.* 1817.

Rothbard, Murray N. *Man, Economy and State.* Los Angeles: Nash Publishing, 1970.

Smith, Adam. *An Inquiry into the Causes and Nature of the Wealth of Nations* (1776).

Spooner, Lysander. *No Treason: The Constitution of No Authority.* Colorado Springs, Colo.: Ralph Myles Publisher, 1973.

Taylor, A.J.P. *The Origins of the Second World War.* New York: Atheneum, 1983.

Turner, I.C.F. *Origins of the First World War*. New York: W. W. Norton, 1970.

United States International Trade Commission. "The Economic Effects of Antidumping and Countervailing Duty Orders and Suspension Agreements." Investigation No. 332-344. Publication 2900. Washington, D.C.: U.S. International Trade Commission, June 1995.

Willett, Thomas D., and Mehrdad Jalalighajar. "U.S. Trade Policy and National Security." *Cato Journal* 3 (winter 1983/84): 717–27.

Strangers in a Strange Land:
The Mitsubishi Sexual Harassment Case

Americans are insular in our approach to the world, intuitively believing that our political system and ethical norms are the best and universalizable, that other countries are hidebound and quaint and their customs odd and distinctly inferior.[1] When we think about the ethics of conducting business abroad, it is usually from our own perspective. We wonder, how can we as Americans engage in commerce with other countries and preserve our moral integrity? How can we remain above the "business as usual" practices of many countries, which may require us to bribe officials, hire "protection" gangs to protect us from themselves and other thugs, entangle ourselves with extortionist governments that oppress their own people, and deal with kleptocrats. Some or all of these practices are temptations or necessities of doing business in most Third World countries, and especially in Russia and other fragments of the former Soviet empire. Western, developed countries, particularly those of the British Commonwealth, naturally pose less of a problem since the customs and politics of the people are "civilized," that is, so much closer to our own.

---

1. The chapter title is borrowed from Robert A. Heinlein, *Stranger in a Strange Land* (New York: Berkley Medallion Book, 1961).

This peculiarly American insularity ensures that we rarely consider the converse proposition, namely, what problems do American culture, law, and politics pose for foreigners doing their "business abroad" in the United States? We seem, to ourselves at least, sensible, sophisticated, and rational when it comes to our values and legal system—no doubt, the "best in the world"—that foreigners are expected to drop their goofy customs and rapidly acquiesce to ours. Despite the recent influence of multiculturalism, this still remains a fair appraisal of typical American attitudes, for multiculturalism has more to do with American racial problems and internal politics than with seeking a deep understanding of alien cultural norms.

For non-Westerners doing business in the United States, however, our customs often seem alien, peculiar, or just plain wrong. Perhaps there is no better example of this culture shock, and its deleterious effect on a large multinational corporation doing business in our country, than Mitsubishi Motor Manufacturing of America's (MMMA's) reaction to two sexual harassment suits, one brought by twenty-nine of its female employees in 1994 and the other by the Equal Employment Opportunity Commission (EEOC) in 1996. (The EEOC is the agency established by the Civil Rights Act of 1964 to investigate charges of discrimination in the workplace on the basis of race, national origin, religion, color, and sex.)

Mitsubishi's belligerent approach to the EEOC's lengthy investigation, its stubborn resistance to the agency's conciliation efforts, its obduracy after the filing of the lawsuits, and especially its very public, in-your-face response to the EEOC's suit raise a strong suspicion that the cultural values of its Japanese leadership played a significant, but difficult to assess, role in its odd behavior. Rather than accommodating the EEOC—by zealously avoiding the harsh glare of media notoriety and its negative effect on the bottom line—Mitsubishi aggressively took on the

EEOC and flaunted its defiance for all the world to witness. American-owned companies know better than this and typically respond passively to the EEOC, in an attempt to avoid adverse publicity and to make the problem go away as quickly as possible.[2] Few American companies wish to push the EEOC to the point of filing a lawsuit (a rare occurrence in any case)[3] and they assiduously avoid ruffling the feathers of EEOC's investigators and litigators. Mitsubishi's handling of a multitude of charges of sexual harassment by female employees on its assembly line stands in marked contrast at every turn to the typical reaction of American corporations. Mitsubishi's Japanese upper management—defiant rather than accommodating, belligerent rather than obsequious, publicity seeking rather than camera shy—made a bad situation distinctly worse.

Remarkable, by American corporate standards, was Mitsubishi's most conspicuous ploy: On April 9, 1996, a mere thirteen days after the EEOC filed its suit in federal district court, Mitsu-

2. As Betty Southland Murphy, former chair of the National Labor Relations Board, observed at the time of the settlement of the Mitsubishi case in June 1988: "Of course, these kinds of national lawsuits can happen to any large corporation, and the key . . . is to resolve the problem quickly and quietly . . . well before a lawsuit is filed, and the press gets involved." "Lessons of Mitsubishi Settlement," *National Law Journal*, June 22, 1988, B5.

3. In fiscal year (FY) 1995, the EEOC filed 315 lawsuits of all employment discrimination types, only a small percentage of which concerned sexual harassment. Ninety-eight percent of employment discrimination cases are handled by private attorneys, rather than the EEOC, which has experienced a huge backlog of cases in the 1990s. "EEOC Flexes New Muscles in Mitsubishi Case, but It Lacks the Bulk to Push Business Around," *Wall Street Journal*, April 29, 1996, A24. Sexual harassment complaints to the EEOC proliferated after the passage of the Civil Rights Act of 1991, which allowed jury trials and, for the first time, awards of compensatory and punitive damages, capped on a sliding scale by the size of employers. Sexual harassment complaints between FY 1991 and FY 1997 went from 6,883 to 15,889. "Sexual Harassment Charges: EEOC & FEPAs Combined: FY 1991–FY 1997," *U.S. Equal Employment Opportunity Commission*, August 11, 1998 (from the EEOC's web site).

bishi's management organized and funded a demonstration by nearly three thousand of its employees in front of the EEOC's regional office in Chicago. MMMA paid for the buses (at a cost of $33,871.10) that transported the employees to Chicago from their workplace in Normal, Illinois; it treated them to lunch at a cost of $15,000; and its chief counsel and "designated official spokesman" helped rally employees to participate. To top it off, employees who participated in the demonstration were paid for a full day of work; those who stayed behind were ordered to report to work or lose a day's pay and spent the day cleaning the plant. From the harsh tone and heated rhetoric in some of the EEOC's subsequent legal pleadings, this extraordinary response did not sit well with the regulators.

Were Mitsubishi's Japanese top managers heroes or fools and knaves? At the time, public reaction was mixed, with feminist groups and Jesse Jackson offering scathing denunciations and organizing a boycott, and a few muted voices (and perchance many more silent ones) evincing mild admiration for Mitsubishi's seemingly courageous stand against a bullying and over-reaching federal regulatory agency. But the EEOC was in no mood to brook another instance of such public opposition, having just been burned by its charges against Hooters, a restaurant chain that flaunts its scantily clad waitresses along with its buffalo wings and fries. In November 1995, after four years of investigation by the EEOC, Hooters went public with its frustrations in dealing with the agency. The EEOC had accused Hooters of sex discrimination in its hiring of waitresses and demanded that $22 million be paid in lost wages to males denied positions as Hooter Girls, that men be hired as waiters, and that sensitivity training be implemented. The company launched a counterattack with a news conference featuring its amply endowed waitresses, charging that if the EEOC succeeded it would jeopardize the employment of its thirteen thousand employees, mostly women.

The chain's media blitz, deriding the EEOC's "nanny state"[4] overreaching, put the EEOC on the defensive. Hooters ran adds featuring a man dressed in a Hooters Girl outfit replete with skimpy shorts, padded bra, blond wig, and a punch line reading "Washington—Get a Grip." Hooter's marketing and public relations consultants festooned billboards with the same message and distributed comment cards on Frisbees to be sent to the EEOC. Hooters succeeded in making the EEOC's position look ridiculous, not the sort of publicity regulatory agencies appreciate, to say the least. Don Livingston, former general counsel of the EEOC, would later comment that Hooters' publicity strategy was well designed, in contrast to Mitsubishi's blundering publicity campaign. "If you're in a case with the EEOC, you are going to attract publicity. If you want to know how to handle a case like that, look at the Mitsubishi case and what they did and do the opposite."[5] On May 2, 1996, in the face of Hooters' adroitly crafted, humorous campaign, the EEOC backed off, claiming that after four years of investigating the chain, its attention could more wisely be spent on other cases and that a private, class action suit by four men denied waitress jobs would suffice.[6] Two years later Hooters would settle that suit for a pittance.[7]

---

4. John Baden, "Perverse Consequences (P.C.) of the Nanny State," *Seattle Times*, January 17, 1996.

5. *The Atlanta Lawyer Journal*, January 10, 1997, relaying comments Livingston made on November 20, 1996, at a labor law luncheon at the Georgia Railroad Depot.

6. "EEOC Drops Hooters Sex-Discrimination Probe," CNN, May 2, 1996 (reporting on a letter from the EEOC received by Rep. Harris Fawell [R., Illinois], a critic of the commission's Hooters investigation and chairman of a House subcommittee on employment).

7. Hooters agreed to a $2 million fund to compensate men denied Hooters Girls positions and agreed to consider men for secondary positions as bartenders

Badly burned by Hooters' adroit public relations campaign, and a scant three weeks before it would give up that fight, the EEOC launched its lawsuit against Mitsubishi. Unaccustomed to open resistance by corporate America, this time the EEOC would not be caught napping and would hit Mitsubishi with a media blitz of its own. The automaker's public relations miscues, coupled with the overwhelming evidence amassed against it by the commission, would salvage the EEOC's public image. Mitsubishi's Japanese executive ranks would be decimated in the process and its reputation tarnished.

Before probing the moral dimensions of the Mitsubishi case, it will be helpful to look at the legal framework of sexual harassment law and the role played by the EEOC in investigating such charges, and to examine the evidence in the EEOC's case against Mitsubishi and the unfolding saga of the company's public response.

Sexual Harassment: The Legal Background

Sexual harassment, as defined by the Equal Employment Opportunity Commission, includes "unwelcome sexual advances, requests for sexual favors, and other verbal or physical conduct of a sexual nature" when that conduct affects an individual's employment, the conditions of employment, unreasonably interferes with work performance, or creates "an intimidating, hostile, or offensive working environment."[8] A more radical variant of the definition of sexual harassment includes a heavy dose of ideology—of men exploiting women—while the EEOC defini-

---

or hosts. Paul A. Driscoll, "Hooters Settles Gender Discrimination Lawsuit, Gets to Keep Waitresses," Associated Press, September 30, 1997.

8. EEOC *Guidelines on Discrimination Because of Sex* (29 C.F.R. §1604.11) (1980).

tion is on its face gender neutral. The radical definition includes the notion of male hegemony over women in the workplace (and society at large) and the use of that power in a sexual guise to subjugate working women.

Federal law on sexual harassment emerged in a curious and totally unanticipated way. When the Civil Rights Act of 1964 passed in a deeply divided Congress, one of its most important and hotly disputed titles, Title VII, prohibited employment discrimination by race, national origin, religion, color, or sex.[9] Sex, however, was added as a hostile amendment by a southern congressman who hoped, thereby, to make the title unpalatable to enough of his colleagues that it would be jettisoned. That ploy did not work, and sex discrimination in employment became, almost accidentally, the target of federal prohibition. The principal objective of both Title VII and the Civil Rights Act in its entirety was to eradicate the long legacy of slavery, segregation, and their remaining effects on African Americans. Women's employment barriers were not really on Congress's radar screen at the time. Even further off the screen in the early sixties was any notion of sexual harassment.

Courts are accustomed to reading congressional tea leaves in their quest to decipher "congressional intent." This judicial device proved utterly barren in sexual harassment cases since Congress had held no discussion on sexual harassment and uttered barely a few sentences on the meaning of the amendment that appended "sex" to what would later be termed Title VII's "pro-

---

9. Title VII's exact language reads:
It shall be an unlawful employment practice for an employer—(1) to fail or refuse to hire or to discharge any individual, or otherwise to discriminate against any individual with respect to his compensation, terms, conditions, or privileges of employment because of such individual's race, color, religion, sex, or national origin.
42 U.S.C. §2000e-2(1982).

tected groups." That sexual harassment would be defined and imported into Title VII's ban on sex discrimination was in no member of Congress's mind in 1964, and "sexual harassment" as a concept would be the work of the next generation: of academic feminists and creative judges. In this sense, sexual harassment as federal law is essentially judge-made law. As the law on Title VII sexual discrimination evolved, sexual harassment became part of the concept but not without some early resistance by the lower federal courts.

Of the early feminist work on developing the concept of sexual harassment, perhaps most influential was that of Catharine A. MacKinnon, an academic lawyer. *Sexual Harassment of Working Women: A Case of Sex Discrimination*,[10] published in 1979, forcefully argued for including sexual harassment in Title VII's prohibition against sex discrimination. This prohibition, developed by the courts, means that the same criteria of selection, compensation, benefits, and advancement opportunities available to men must also be available to women. MacKinnon's views on the relationship between men and women—in which she saw sexual harassment as a metaphor for capitalism's exploitation of women by men—were filtered through Marxist glasses. For her, Marx's capitalists exploiting their workers were replaced by men exploiting women. Men in positions of power throughout society, and particularly in the workplace, impose a "group injury" of sexual harassment on women because they are women and not because of their individual qualities. As feminists are fond of pointing out, sexual harassment is about power, as is rape, not about sexual desire. MacKinnon's essential message was that men, who are in the driver's seat in corporate America, use their favored position in the capitalist system to

---

10. Catharine A. MacKinnon, *Sexual Harassment of Working Women: A Case of Sex Discrimination* (New Haven: Yale University Press, 1979).

dominate and control the lives of women. A radical feminist, she saw marriage as tantamount to prostitution and sexual harassment as the vehicle for prostituting women in the workplace. When a woman is fired from her job for refusing the sexual advances of her supervisor, it is *because she is a woman* and not because of the personal sexual peccadilloes of her boss—this is the MacKinnon teaching, and the courts soon became her apt pupils, but only after some expressions of skepticism.

In the mid-1970s, judges who heard the earliest cases alleging sexual harassment as a component of Title VII's ban on sex discrimination in employment were reluctant to read into the non-existent congressional record any intent to incorporate even the most blatant scenarios of sexual harassment. These judges, mostly serving on federal district courts, rejected a category of sexually harassing behavior that would come to be termed *quid pro quo sexual harassment*. Typically, this involves a supervisor who uses his position of authority over an employee to exact or attempt to exact sexual favors in return for promotion or other job-related benefits or who threatens job detriments if the employee does not oblige. These types of cases—now considered the most serious instances of sexual harassment—would be the first accepted by the courts, but the initial cases met with nearly unanimous rebuke. Judges expressed reluctance to hold employers liable for what they saw as the essentially personal sexual overtures of their managers. One judge wrote that the verbal and sexual conduct that triggered the resignations of two female employees was "nothing more than a personal proclivity, peculiarity or mannerism . . . satisfying a personal urge. Certainly no employer policy is here involved."[11] Since sexual discrimination suits up to that point had involved company policies, the judge was hard pressed to see how sexual proposals by a supervisor

---

11. *Corne v. Bausch & Lomb* 399 F. Supp. 161 (D. Ariz. 1975).

could do anything but hurt the company. Under Title VII it is employers who are held liable for the infractions of their supervisory employees, as agents of the company, and judges had great difficulty seeing how quid pro quo sexual overtures fit within the "scope of employment"[12] of managers, particularly when judges assumed that companies could only be hurt by such activities.

In 1976, however, the District of Columbia district court would reject this trend and looked favorably for the first time on a quid pro quo case. In *Williams v. Saxbe*,[13] the judge reasoned that a woman who was dismissed for declining the sexual advances of her supervisor suffered from a *rule* (that is, an act that functioned in effect as an employer policy) that created an artificial barrier to the employment of the female gender but not the male. This rule analogy made sexual harassment charges look more like the standard sex discrimination suits over employer policies that favored men over women, to which the courts had become accustomed. The judge, then, concluded that this was enough to make the supervisor's acts the acts of the employer; this case set the precedent for future sexual harassment cases.

Supervisors, however, are not the only men in the workplace who can discomfit women. In the early 1980s, the courts were presented with cases in which women argued that their coworkers created a "hostile environment" by sexually laden comments, exhibitionistic acts, unwanted touches, telephone calls, and threatening remarks and behavior. (In later years, lewd jokes and

---

12. "Scope of employment" is a standard way of assessing whether an employee is acting in the company's behalf when an act of negligence occurs. The same "agency principles" were transported from tort law into interpreting Title VII transgressions by employees. *Restatement (Second) of Agency* §219 (1958). The Supreme Court would later endorse this approach in its first sexual harassment case, *Meritor Savings Bank v. Vinson*, 477 U.S. 57 (1986).

13. 413 F. Supp. 654 (D.D.C. 1976).

pinups would be added to the list.) These complaints usually alleged psychological injury as a result of such episodes, although many plaintiffs contended that they were forced to quit their jobs when they could not stand the behavior any longer. Since such experiences did not fall within the newly developed quid pro quo scenario—since coworkers were involved rather than supervisors—plaintiffs' attorneys argued for the expansion of sexual harassment to include *hostile environment* claims, much like the hostile environment claims that the courts had already looked favorably upon in Title VII racial discrimination cases. The courts quickly obliged.[14] Employers would be held responsible for the unwelcome (in the sense that the victim did nothing to solicit or incite the conduct and found it offensive or undesirable) sexual harassment perpetrated by its employees if the harassment affected a "term, condition, or privilege or employment" and if the employer knew or should have known of the harassment and failed to take prompt remedial action. Supervisors can commit "hostile environment" sexual harassment as well as coworkers, if the supervisor's actions do not amount to a threat, as in a quid pro quo case, but are similar to the harassing activities that coworkers perpetrate.

Employers in quid pro quo cases are held to a "strict liability" standard, that is, if it is proven that the supervisor committed the act, then the employer is responsible because the supervisor is considered the agent of the employer. In *hostile environment* cases the standard is more akin to a negligence standard, where the plaintiff must show that the employer "knew" of the act (because the victim informed the employer) or that the employer "should have known" (because the harassment was so pervasive that it

14. The leading case, until the Supreme Court decided its first case in 1986, was the Eleventh Circuit Appeals Court's *Henson v. City of Dundee*, 682 F. 2d 897 (11th Cir. 1982).

gives rise to an inference of employer knowledge) and failed to take prompt remedial action. Employers can defend themselves against hostile environment charges by arguing that the harassment did not in fact occur, that if it did it was trivial and transitory, or that the company took effective action to stop it. Entering the fray late in the game, the Supreme Court decided its first sexual harassment case in 1986, a hostile environment case, and merely gave its official imprimatur to what had been transpiring in the lower federal courts for a decade. The high Court, however, declined to establish a definitive standard for employer liability in hostile environment cases perpetrated by supervisors, instructing the lower courts to employ standard agency principles.[15] This liability standard would not be settled by the Supreme Court until 1998, when it decided two such cases, but this would come some thirteen days after the charges against Mitsubishi had been settled.[16]

15. This led to a difference of opinion among the circuit courts over whether employers should be held to a strict liability standard for *hostile environment* sexual harassment by supervisors (the minority view) or whether prompt remedial action should exonerate an employer (the majority view). See "Remedial Actions Limit an Employer's Liability," *National Law Journal* 18, no. 26 (February 26, 1996): C20.

16. Between *Meritor v. Vinson* in 1986 and the two cases in 1998, the Supreme Court decided one other "hostile environment" case, *Harris v. Forklift Systems, Inc.*, 510 U.S. 17 (1993). In that case, brought by a woman who complained that the insults and sexual innuendos directed against her by the company's president created an abusive environment, the Court decided that a woman did not have to suffer serious psychological harm or economic injury in order to make out a case of *hostile environment* sexual harassment. Courts must consider not just the psychological effect on the plaintiff but the severity of the conduct, whether it is threatening or humiliating, and whether it unreasonably interferes with the employee's performance at work. This decision signaled an expanding sympathy for sexual harassment complaints by the Court.

The Supreme Court actually decided four sexual harassment cases in 1998, but only two of them are relevant to the standard-of-liability issue that the Court had left open in *Meritor*. The other two dealt with a sexual relationship between a teacher and a high school student, and the harassment of a man by other

Sexual harassment became a cause célèbre in 1991, when law professor Anita Hill accused Supreme Court nominee Judge Clarence Thomas of sexually harassing her while she worked under his direction as a special assistant at the Department of Education and later at the EEOC, when Thomas became its chairman. When Hill's confidential complaint to the Senate Judiciary Committee was leaked to the press, just two days before Thomas's nomination was scheduled for final Senate vote, the hearings were reopened and Hill's charges given a full public airing. Hill accused Thomas of making numerous sexually provocative remarks to her about X-rated movies, of requesting dates with her on several occasions despite her refusals, and of making offensive, sexually loaded comments to her. Judge Thomas maintained that he was mystified by her charges and that their rela-

---

heterosexual men; respectively, they are *Gebser v. Lago Vista Independent School District*, 118 S.Ct. 1989 (1998), and *Oncale v. Sundowner Offshore Services*, 118 S.Ct. 998 (1998). The two relevant cases, handed down on the same day, are *Faragher v. City of Boca Raton*, 118 S.Ct. 2275 (1998), and *Ellerth v. Burlington Industries, Inc.*, 118 S.Ct. 2365 (1998). Both cases raised the issue of "vicarious liability" of an employer for the sexually harassing conduct of its supervisor, when that conduct falls under the *hostile environment* rubric, when the victim was not fired, and when the employer was not informed by the victim of the behavior of her supervisor(s). The Court decided that the employer is "vicariously liable" (that is, the victim does not have to prove negligence on the part of the employer) but that the employer can defend itself when the victim has not suffered any job detriment at the hands of the harasser. The employer can mount what is termed an "affirmative defense," showing that it exercised reasonable care to prevent and correct any offensive sexual behavior and that the complaining employee failed to take advantage of any preventive or corrective opportunity provided by the company. The employer, on the contrary, is "strictly liable" when the supervisor's harassment leads to the discharge, demotion, or undesirable transfer of the victim; the employer, in other words, has no defense once retribution of these sorts has been proven. Employers were generally pleased with these decisions, for they established a more-or-less "bright line" defense for employers if they have instituted a sexual harassment policy, informed employees of its existence, established a complaint mechanism that circumvents the harassing supervisor, and investigated and taken prompt remedial action.

tionship had been one of mentor and protégée. The televised hearings, although ultimately inconclusive, provided a virtual teach-in on sexual harassment. Thomas vigorously denied the charges, and a parade of witnesses, mostly female subordinates, testified to his sterling character. Hill's witnesses were unable to directly corroborate her charges. In the end, Thomas was confirmed as an associate justice to the Supreme Court by a fifty-two to forty-eight vote in the Senate, the slimmest margin of victory in American history.

In 1991 Congress passed a new Civil Rights Act that sweetened the pot for sex discrimination plaintiffs, including those charging sexual harassment. The act expanded remedies available under federal civil rights law, so that victorious plaintiffs are no longer limited to receiving back pay, reinstatement, or promotion but may now recover compensatory damages and, more significantly, punitive damages (although damages are capped at $300,000 per victim for the largest employers). In 1992, in the aftermath of the Hill/Thomas hearings, sexual harassment complaints to the EEOC increased by 53 percent.[17] Between 1992 and 1993, total awards in sexual harassment complaints handled

17. In FY1991, the EEOC received 6,883 charges and 10,532 in FY1992. By FY1997, the number of new claims had escalated to 15,889. Monetary benefits obtained for complainants by the EEOC went from $7.1 million in 1991 to $49.5 million in FY1997 (both figures exclude monetary awards that resulted from litigation). Only a tiny percentage of complaints result in court cases, either by individuals or, even more rarely, by the EEOC. In FY1997, for example, 41 percent of the charges resulted in an EEOC finding of "no reasonable cause" after investigation, another 39.7 percent were dismissed by "administrative closure" (which means that the charging party could not be located, failed to respond to EEOC communications, refused to accept full relief, etc.). The rest were settled, successfully conciliated, or withdrawn with benefits, except for 2.9 percent, which were classified as "unsuccessful conciliations" (the category from which EEOC considers litigation). "Sexual Harassment Charges: EEOC & FEPA's Combined: FY1991–FY1997" (the figures include cases filed with Fair Employment Practice agencies throughout the country; in many states these agencies are the first avenue of complaint, and they work closely with the EEOC).

internally by the EEOC doubled.[18] When supplemented by state charges under various tort theories, sexual harassment suits can bring jury awards into the millions. In this highly charged atmosphere the first complaint against Mitsubishi was filed, in November 1992, by a woman complaining of sexual harassment going back to the opening of the factory in 1987. Perhaps this filing, and the others that soon followed, was coincidental, but the notoriety attached to the Hill/Thomas hearings probably encouraged the women who had long suffered in anonymity at the Mitsubishi plant to seek legal redress.

By the time that the first charges against Mitsubishi were leveled, corporate America had come to understand the supercharged environment surrounding sexual overtures and innuendo in the office and the plant. EEOC *Guidelines* dating back to 1980, as well as numerous lawsuits, incessant bombardment by consultants, and the Hill/Thomas hearings, had put employers on notice that sexual harassment could place their companies in serious jeopardy, both through litigation and in the court of public opinion. Consultants repeatedly warned employers that there was no foolproof way to insulate themselves from such suits or to avoid losing them if they ever came to trial (a relative rarity) or to avoid settling them at considerable cost (a more common outcome). Employers were also on notice that there were some surefire ways of increasing the likelihood of a bad outcome: Not having a sexual harassment policy at all was a sure loser (even clueless Mitsubishi had a written sexual harassment policy). Not publicizing to employees that one had a policy and what it involved was another clear loser. Not having an effective complaint procedure was, likewise, a foolish blunder. Requiring putative victims of sexual harassment to complain up the chain of command, which often would mean complaining to the harasser,

18. Ibid.

was also a definite nonstarter. A complaint procedure involving a designated person removed from line management was the favored course, and completing an impartial, confidential, and speedy investigation was the sine qua non. Taking effective remedial action to stop the harassment—removing the harassed employee from the supervision of the harasser or from the locale of her harassing coworkers or warning, reprimanding, or even firing the harasser(s)—was the gold standard. As we will see in the next section, Mitsubishi fell short on practically every one of these counts.

Mitsubishi also presumably knew that foreign companies doing business in the United States are subject to Title VII's various prohibitions against employment discrimination, including sexual harassment. According to EEOC guidelines:

> By employing individuals within the United States, a foreign employer invokes the benefits and protections of U.S. law. As a result, the employer should reasonably anticipate being subjected to the Title VII enforcement process should any charge of discrimination arise directly from the business the employer does in the United States.[19]

---

19. "EEOC: Enforcement Guidance on Application of Title VII and ADA to Conduct Overseas and to Foreign Employers in the United States," issued October 20, 1993, superseding a September 2, 1988, policy statement. The only exception to this coverage is if a treaty or binding international agreement bars application of U.S. antidiscrimination statutes to a foreign company. This was not an issue in the Mitsubishi case. Friendship Commerce and Navigation (FCN) treaties are the usual avenue of escape by treaty. However, as the EEOC points out, a case decided in 1982 by the Supreme Court held that an FCN treaty between the United States and Japan did not exempt an American-incorporated subsidiary of a Japanese company from Title VII but did exempt Japanese-incorporated companies doing business in the United States. (FCN treaties only allow foreign companies to hire their own nationals for executive and management positions and would not insulate them from charges of sexual harassment, in any case.) This was a decision, presumably, that Mitsubishi's counsel were familiar with (*Sumitomo Shaji America, Inc. v. Avigliano*, 457 U.S. 176, 1982). The

Mitsubishi did in fact have a sexual harassment policy and an enforcement mechanism, but both were woefully inadequate and, in any event, recognized more in the breach than in the observance.

The EEOC's Case Against Mitsubishi

Barely three weeks after the EEOC filed its sexual harassment suit against Mitsubishi, on April 9, 1996, after a four-year investigation of the company, Astra USA, another foreign-owned subsidiary operating in the United States, faced a sexual harassment allegation.[20] The reactions of the two companies could not have been more different: Mitsubishi reacted with rare obduracy, even belligerence, through long, drawn-out negotiations with the EEOC preceding the lawsuit, with defiance once the suit was filed, and with a nightmarish public relations strategy that only exacerbated the damage to the company and infuriated the EEOC; Astra USA, in contrast, acted preemptively to diffuse the situation before the charges could spiral completely out of control.

When Astra USA, a Massachusetts subsidiary of the Swedish pharmaceutical company Astra AB, learned that *Business Week*

1993 *Guidance* cites cases back to 1988 on this point. The 1991 Civil Rights Act overturned a 1991 Supreme Court decision that declined to apply Title VII to cover American citizens working for an American-owned company abroad, but did not affect the issue that concerns us, namely, foreign companies doing business in the United States, which had always been subject to U.S. law.

20. This account of the EEOC's charges against Mitsubishi and the company's reaction to them is taken largely from the EEOC's brief in response to Mitsubishi's filing for partial summary judgment (filed September 15, 1997 in United States District Court for the Central District of Illinois, Peoria Division, Case No. 96-1192) (henceforth referred to as EEOC Memorandum), the consent decree signed by Mitsubishi and the EEOC that concluded the legal proceedings (filed June 11, 1998 to the same court), and various newspaper accounts from around the country (from a Lexis/Nexis search).

was about to publish allegations of sexual harassment against its president and chief executive, Lars Bildman, its board acted swiftly, voting to suspend Bildman, a Swede, from his positions, despite fifteen years of service as chief executive in the American operation. A vice president for sales and marketing was also suspended, and three other managers resigned. The parent company learned of the charges when an investigative journalist began interviewing executives. Astra immediately sent senior executives to consult with people at its U.S. company and then instigated a preliminary investigation, which culminated in the suspension. Following that action, the company launched a formal investigation, conducted by outside legal counsel in addition to its own people. Although Astra USA's American spokesman insisted that the Swedish company was not prompted by Mitsubishi's predicament and that it would never tolerate sexual harassment in any case, he added that "the Mitsubishi case has given companies around the world a heightened awareness" of the importance of dealing with sexual harassment charges in the United States.[21]

Astra AB's and Astra USA's reactions doubtlessly cheered the EEOC and encouraged it to think that its massive assault on Mitsubishi was paying immediate and direct benefits. Perhaps, too, Swedes might be more sensitive to American mores, having a shared Western culture, values, and social sensibilities, and greater familiarity with American ways of doing business. Astra AB tried to staunch a potentially costly and embarrassing public relations fiasco that could have negatively affected its thriving U.S. operations. Although the company quickly put in place its

21. "Companies and Finance: The Americas: Astra Suspends Head of U.S. Operations," *Financial Times* (London), April 30, 1996; "Sexual-Harassment Cases Trip Up Foreign Companies," *Wall Street Journal*, May 9, 1996; "Astra Chief Suspended after Harassment Charge: Westborough Firm to Probe Employee Allegations," *Boston Globe*, April 30, 1996.

damage-control strategy, its approach circumscribed but did not eliminate the damage: Several private suits alleging sexual harassment by top officials of Astra USA were filed; the EEOC alleged a widespread pattern of such abuse at the company; the president was eventually terminated, accused of embezzlement of company funds, tried and sentenced to twenty-one months of incarceration, and sued by Astra for recompense; and, finally, Astra settled EEOC charges, in February 1998, by agreeing to pay $9.85 million in damages and have its sexual harassment policies monitored for two years. The EEOC had contended that seventy-nine women and one man had been the victims of sexual harassment by thirty men and that the men at the top set a bad example that had percolated down management ranks. Astra's $9.85 million settlement dwarfed the EEOC's previous record of $1.3 million in a sexual harassment charge but would itself be dwarfed by the Mitsubishi settlement two months later. Astra's new management cooperated with the EEOC throughout its investigation and cleaned out its entire senior management. At the time that the company settled with the EEOC, the new chief executive said, "As a company we are ashamed of the unacceptable behavior that took place. To each person who suffered, I offer our apologies."[22]

Mitsubishi could have done what Astra USA did when the first complaints were lodged separately by four women with the EEOC in 1992, or even earlier, when it first began receiving complaints from women of sexual harassment at its Normal, Illinois, plant. Instead, over a four-year period before the EEOC filed suit, and for two years afterward, until the company entered settlement talks with the commission, the company did everything in its power to make its plight worse and to provoke the EEOC. If

22. "Firm to Pay $10 Million in Settlement of Sex Case," *New York Times*, February 6, 1998, p. A10.

we retrace Mitsubishi's missteps we will see how a foreign-owned American corporation got itself into such a morass, seemingly throwing caution and good business sense to the winds at every opportunity.

In a lengthy memorandum (filed on September 15, 1996, with the United States District Court for the Central District of Illinois, Peoria Division, the court in which the EEOC filed its case against Mitsubishi on April 9, 1996), the EEOC gave its most complete and publicly accessible description of its charges and evidence against the company. The opening statement indicates the extent to which Mitsubishi had managed over the previous four years to outrage the EEOC, for the memorandum exhibits polemic intemperance seldom found in pleadings by government agencies.[23] This is a case, the EEOC stated, about the

> infection of a huge, state-of-the-art automobile manufacturing plant with the poison of discrimination. The discrimination challenged by EEOC is Mitsubishi's creation and toleration of a sexually hostile and abusive work environment in flagrant violation of federal law [sic]. The already available evidence indicates that the magnitude and scope of sexual and sex-based harassment at Mitsubishi, and the degree of managerial complicity therein, are unprecedented.[24]

23. The EEOC's Memorandum characterized Mitsubishi's arguments in support of its motion for partial summary judgment as "dead wrong" (p. 3). Mitsubishi's argument to the court that the EEOC couldn't pursue the charges as a "pattern or practice" case was met in part by this remark by the EEOC: "If any sexual harassment case has ever involved a 'pattern or practice' of discrimination under Title VII, this one does" (p. 3). Later, at p. 61, the EEOC declared that "Mitsubishi has sought to bury its head in the sand when it came to sexual harassment claims and then scream lack of notice despite overwhelming evidence to the contrary."

24. EEOC Memorandum, September 15, 1997, p. 1.

The EEOC then proceeded to categorize five major types of sexual harassment that they had gathered evidence about from some three hundred female employees (of the eight hundred employed at the company). In all, the EEOC maintained, four hundred different male employees at the company (out of thirty-two hundred) had engaged in various acts of harassment. This widespread pattern of abuse, the EEOC argued, and the company's obduracy, had prompted the commission to file a "pattern and practice" case against the company, an unusual type of case for the agency to file over sexual harassment allegations but not unprecedented.[25] Pattern and practice cases are usually reserved for racial discrimination cases or, less often, sex discrimination cases, where a company exhibits endemic, widespread discrimination that affects a large category of employees or its official policies adversely affect a group of employees protected by Title VII. Pattern or practice cases are rare in sexual harassment allegations because complaints are usually received from one or a few employees; where more are involved, companies usually accede to EEOC conciliation efforts, and charges never get as far as the courts. The widespread nature of the complaints and the number of women affected, combined with Mitsubishi's truculence, drove the EEOC to mount the massive assault a pattern or practice case involves.

The EEOC argued that five main types of sexual harassment, "individually and together," created a hostile working environment for women at the Mitsubishi plant, as follows: (1) At Mitsubishi's new employee orientation women were "characterized as inferior." Managers sent to Japan for training visited "audience participation" sex bars at which the Japanese hosts and

---

25. The EEOC would later make the same type of allegation against Astra USA: that the company exhibited a "pattern or practice" of widespread sexual harassment.

American trainees participated in sex acts with prostitutes on stage. (2) Women being instructed on Japanese culture were told that they were unwelcome in the plant; that the Japanese did not consider women suitable employees in manufacturing operations; that women risked being regarded as flirtatious if they made eye contact with their Japanese managers or touched a Japanese man on the shoulder; and that women's conditions of work were less favorable than those of male employees. (3) The factory was infested with a "sexualized environment": Women were subjected to sexual graffiti affixed to cars as they moved down the line; to "sexual comments, objects, and gestures demonstrating sexual organs and positions." Women were called "cunt," "whore," "bitch," and their sex lives were openly debated. Male employees exposed themselves to women. (4) Male workers and managers came to the plant with pornographic pictures, which they shared with others. Some of the pictures showed Japanese executives and American managers and employees engaging in sex acts at after-hour sex parties at local hotels. The parties, which were organized on company time by managers, included prostitutes who, for a fee, allowed revelers to lick whipped cream off their breasts and pluck cherries from their vaginas with their teeth. (5) Finally, women were subjected to both physical and verbal attacks, including threatening phone calls, assaults in cars, unwanted touching and rubbing, and other lewd behavior.

The sex parties, organized by company managers on company time, were a particularly insidious element of Mitsubishi's plant culture, the EEOC contended, and the company only investigated and took mild action against participants on the eve of the EEOC's filing of its lawsuit, in February and March 1996. EEOC contended that even this late and lame response was prompted by a desire to create a paper trail for future legal wrangling, not by a genuine desire to extinguish a practice that had company acquiescence and participation from the executive ranks on down. Japanese coordinators, a managerial level above unit group leaders and branch managers, participated in these escapades, as Mitsubishi's own belated investigation corroborated. One unit group leader, when asked why he did not stop the circulation of pictures from these parties on the plant floor, responded that "[he] did not think of [the photographs] in terms of being offensive and said he looked at them as the same as guys coming in after a hunting trip and showing pictures of the deer."[26] Women who complained of finding such pictures in their desk drawers were threatened with losing their jobs; while one woman stated that she did not complain because "It would be difficult to complain to the supervisors that queued up in line to see [the photographs]." Mitsubishi's investigation showed that branch managers assumed that the sex parties were standard operating procedure at the company since high-level Japanese technical advisers requested and participated in them and were pictured licking women's breasts in the pictures circulating around the plant. Sex parties were also organized to accommodate visiting Japanese executives. All disciplinary agreements with the managers involved in the sex parties, which were signed the day after the EEOC filed suit, merely placed the offenders on probation, warning them that they might be penalized for future infractions. All had received merit increases after their interviews and write-ups and before signing these disciplinary "last chance agreements." No immediate disciplinary penalties ensued. The company's obtuseness is also reflected in the fact that the sex parties continued even while the company was denying their existence in the face of a private sexual harassment lawsuit filed by twenty-nine female employees in 1994.[27] (That

26. EEOC Memorandum, p. 36.
27. *Evans, Paz, et al. v. Mitsubishi*, C.D. Illinois (Peoria Div.) No. 94-1545 (Judge

lawsuit would eventually be settled in August 1997, in the midst of proceedings on the EEOC case against Mitsubishi, for $9.5 million.)

Women who complained of sexually demeaning incidents—and many did, despite the company's ineffective complaint

---

Mihm). Ms. Paz was the first woman who to file a complaint with the EEOC in November 1992. She was followed by approximately thirty other women. Private parties can file suit under Title VII if they first receive a "right to sue" notice from the EEOC. Ms. Paz requested such a letter after the EEOC had not acted on her complaint within the 180-day period specified under Title VII. (The EEOC had huge backlogs and could not proceed on the complaints in a timely fashion.) Paz and twenty-eight other women filed their consolidated suit against the company in 1994. The EEOC would intervene in the *Evans, Paz* sexual harassment and sex discrimination suit in December 1996. This suit is separate from the EEOC's own "pattern and practice" suit, although the charges filed by the women with the EEOC precipitated the commission's wider investigation of the company.

The EEOC continued to investigate the charges against Mitsubishi after it issued Ms. Paz her right to sue letter. On April 19, 1994, the EEOC issued a Commissioner's Charge, of which the company was notified, and instituted its own comprehensive investigation of the employment conditions for women at Mitsubishi. (A Commissioner's Charge is a vehicle for the EEOC to investigate a company when a commissioner decides that there is reasonable cause to believe that a company has engaged in employment discrimination.) That investigation included tours of the company, interviews with 150 employees and former employees, and the collection of documents. On August 9, 1995, the EEOC issued a Letter of Determination finding reasonable cause that the allegations included in its Commissioner's Charge were true. Once the commission finds "reasonable cause," the affected company enters a thirty-day conciliation period with the EEOC in an attempt to resolve the charges. Mitsubishi did this, but the talks broke down in September 1995. The company's general counsel stated in his address to company employees after the EEOC filed suit in April 1996 that the company had expected the EEOC to sue (statement made at the meeting at Mitsubishi [second shift], April 12, 1996). According to the EEOC Memorandum, Mitsubishi met each of the commission's settlement terms with a declaration that it was unnecessary and that it would not comply until the EEOC proved that it was necessary. The company also refused to offer any monetary relief: all in all, a response that the EEOC characterized as "intransigent" (EEOC Memorandum, p. 64).

mechanism and its discouragement of complaints[28]—were frequently subject to retaliation. Mitsubishi's sexual harassment policy required women to report first to their supervisors, who were frequently the very people that they wished to complain about, and then to the Employee Relations Department (ER), which the EEOC claimed behaved ineptly in its handling of charges. Nearly half the declarations from women that the EEOC gathered complained of harassment by supervisors. One supervisor earned the sobriquet "Chester the Molester" for his harassment of new female hires; another told a new female employee that "she belonged to him" during her probationary period. Others told newly hired women that they should be at home "cooking for a husband"; others consigned women to "knee jobs" without giving them the same training that men were given.

Supervisors, even when not the target of the women's complaints, discouraged women from pursuing their grievances. One group leader told a woman who complained about a notorious harasser that "this is a factory. If you don't like it, go sling hamburgers."[29] Another woman requested that she not be paired with her harasser. Her request was denied, her supervisor claimed that if she were moved everyone else would want similar treatment. Employee Relations proved no more helpful, and her travails culminated in her harasser starting the line after she had fainted on it, endangering her physically.[30]

Following Japanese organizational theory, the plant's union-

---

28. The EEOC submitted declarations by sixty women, many of whom did complain, following the company's announced procedures (EEOC Memorandum, p. 26). Complaints by individual employees of Mitsubishi's were presented to the court by the EEOC under seal along with the Memorandum, in order to protect the women's privacy, and cannot be released by the court.

29. Ibid.

30. Ibid.

ized employees are grouped in units of fifteen to thirty employees (associates), and each unit is supervised by a unit group
leader who, in turn, reports to a branch manager. These close
quarters seemed to exacerbate the misery of those women who
reported instances of sexual harassment, for the cursory investigations conducted by Employee Relations sometimes involved
calling in the accused employee or supervisor to confront his
accuser, leaking complaints to other team members, or advising
the entire work group that a woman had complained. This led to
"ostracism and retaliation" against the women, rather than a
remedy, the EEOC alleged. Women who nevertheless persisted
in their complaints to Employee Relations were typically met by
"skepticism, hostility, and an inability or unwillingness to address the problem," according to the EEOC.[31] One victim complained to Employee Relations four times about a male associate;
after the first complaint he made remarks about "getting that
bitch" and "kicking her ass." He was reassigned only after her
fourth complaint and the complaints of other women and after
menacing her by her car. When the company did, on rare occasions, find cause for complaint against a particular male employee, disciplinary action consisted of having him watch a
thirty-minute video on sexual harassment and placing a memo
in his file but typically not one including a finding of sexual
harassment. "Watching the video," the EEOC informed the
court, "became a companywide joke, a badge of honor."[32] A
branch manager received a promotion after ER received a complaint that he had made the "jack off" gesture in sight of thirty
employees. ER investigated complaints that an employee had
exposed himself by interviewing coworkers on the line "*in his
presence*"; the complaints were withdrawn after the man intimi-

31. Ibid., p. 28.
32. Ibid., p. 29.

dated the complainants.[33] Even when ER's investigation found complaints legitimate, the women were often placed in a worse situation. EEOC found this example "particularly shocking": a branch manager (a higher-level supervisory position) sexually assaulted a woman whom he was driving home because she was ill. When her group leader corroborated the story and the branch manager's denials were found unconvincing, ER recommended that he be removed from any supervisory position, but that recommendation was completely ignored.[34]

Mitsubishi, in short, had no effective program of progressive discipline for harassers: no suspension, demotion, docking of pay, or denials of promotion. As of April 1994, when the EEOC filed its Commissioner's Charge against the company,[35] EEOC could find only three instances in which associates had been terminated for sexual harassment. The EEOC's Memorandum was dismissive of Mitsubishi's efforts since that date, and its claim to have dismissed fifteen employees on these grounds, finding the company's response too little and too late and prompted only by "the media breathing down its neck."[36]

Victims who went beyond these ineffective company policies and submitted complaints to the EEOC were, not surprisingly, met by ostracism and, the EEOC charged, retaliation by coworkers encouraged by Mitsubishi management. When twenty-nine women who had submitted grievances to the EEOC filed a private lawsuit against the company in December 1994, the company informed employees that the complaints were "vicious lies" and that the suit could cost men their jobs. Mitsubishi also allowed the bulletin boards to be festooned with "derogatory

33. Ibid. (emphasis in original).
34. Ibid., p. 30.
35. See note 27 for an explanation of Commissioner's Charge.
36. EEOC Memorandum, p. 25.

and defamatory statements" about the women. Management, the EEOC argued, was complicit in "fostering and maintaining" this hostile work environment for women, and it characterized Mitsubishi's managerial practices in this regard as "appalling."[37] Meeting the Seventh Circuit's (the appeals court that covers the state of Illinois) standard for company liability for hostile environment sexual harassment, the EEOC argued, should be a breeze since the EEOC, even at this preliminary stage of the case's progress, had amassed an overwhelming case, even without full discovery and interviews with alleged harassers and ER personnel. That standard, following the Supreme Court's *Meritor v. Vinson* guidance, holds a company liable for hostile environment sexual harassment by supervisors and employees if it "knew or should have known of the harassment and failed to take adequate steps to prevent it."[38] The EEOC's Memorandum exuded supreme confidence on this score.

From the time that the EEOC received its first complaint against Mitsubishi, in November 1992, to the filing of a private lawsuit by twenty-nine female employees in December 1994, the company had been on notice that it had a serious problem that had escaped the bounds of company control. Throughout what would become a long and public ordeal, the company's consistent response was to deny the charges, stonewall, and drag its feet. When faced with the EEOC "pattern and practice" case and the attendant publicity, Mitsubishi summoned its troops to stand in defiance in front of the EEOC's Chicago offices in a massive demonstration, some three thousand strong, organized and paid for by the company. One day after the EEOC filed suit, the company's chairman and its president distributed a letter to employees characterizing their reaction to the suit as one of "abso-

37. Ibid., p. 23.
38. Ibid.

lute denial" of all the commission's sexual harassment allegations, contending that the company had an effective sexual harassment policy. "MMMA," the two wrote in somewhat obscure English, "cannot allow allegations of political and monetary motivation to dampen our morale or efforts."[39]

At one of the pep rallies that the company's American vice president/general counsel organized to marshal employee support, he called the EEOC's charges an "attack" by a government agency. The vice president of Human Resources, also an American, termed the charges "totally unacceptable" and an "outrageous action taken by the EEOC."[40] Employees were urged by the general counsel (the company's official spokesman) to use any and all avenues to sway public opinion in the company's favor: talk shows, letters to the editor, grass roots petitions, the Internet, phone banks, letters to members of Congress, and a demonstration. A credit union account had been set up to pay for an ad by women employees praising the company, he announced. He repeatedly intoned that the "management is not doing this" and that the media blitz would fail if it were suspected that management was manipulating the employees. A few moments later, however, he uttered these words: "The way we get through this is that we win. We've got to win the media by parading thousands strong in Chicago—we'll paint Chicago maroon that day." The clumsy performance culminated in a request for feedback on his performance and the company's predicament, to be placed in suggestion boxes, with the plea that anonymous submissions be labeled M or W or B or G to let him

39. From the April 10, 1996, letter of Chairman and CEO Tsuneo Ohinouye and President and COO Takahisa Komoto addressed to MMMA employees. What the two Japanese executives meant was that the EEOC had political motivations in lodging their charges and that the women whom they represented had monetary aspirations.

40. Meeting at Mitsubishi, April 12, 1996.

know the gender of the author. At the conclusion of the meeting, one questioner asked to see a cartoon that had been handed to the general counsel and was circulating at the meeting. In the cartoon figure's hand was a handbook that said Mitsubishi does not tolerate sexual harassment; when opened, the handbook revealed a centerfold. The general counsel identified the man in the cartoon as "me." Needless to say, the EEOC did not find the cartoon or the general counsel's response amusing. The EEOC charged that retaliation against women intensified after the meeting, with one woman receiving a death threat. Mitsubishi's legal maneuvering in response to the EEOC lawsuit was similarly maladroit, arguing that it had an effective sexual harassment policy and complaint procedure and that it lacked sufficient notice by employees of sexual harassment problems.

The company's ham-handed response unleashed a maelstrom of bad publicity and outrage from women's and civil rights groups. In the immediate aftermath of the demonstration in front of EEOC's Chicago headquarters, Congresswoman Patricia Shroeder and nine of her female colleagues issued a letter reproaching the company for its practices and for retaliating against the women who had filed the charges. On May 1, 1996, the congresswoman and six others requested that the EEOC seek a court order to stop Mitsubishi from such retaliation. John J. Sweeney, president of the AFL-CIO, also condemned the demonstration, stating that management's organization of it "depriv[ed] the women who have brought charges against them of their right to due process free of intimidation." Other commentators marveled at the "in-your-face response" of the company to the EEOC's suit, calling the company's actions unprecedented. On May 7, the Reverend Jesse Jackson and his PUSH/Rainbow coalition called for a boycott of Mitsubishi's automobiles; Patricia Ireland, then president of the National Organization for Women (NOW), announced that her group would picket some

Mitsubishi dealerships.[41] In July 1996, Jesse Jackson went to the parent company's headquarters in Japan to pursue his campaign against Mitsubishi, on racial as well as sexual harassment grounds; on his return to the United States, he vowed to rekindle his efforts against the company's practices.[42]

On April 25, three days after the ill-fated demonstration, the company's Japanese chairman and chief executive, Tsuneo Ohinouye, told the *New York Times* that the company was interested in settling, had been from the beginning, and had "no intention to attack the EEOC or fight the EEOC." Mitsubishi's general counsel, however, continued denying that the company had settlement in mind, and the EEOC averred that the company had not contacted the commission about a willingness to settle.[43] In mid-May, in an attempt to stem the rising tide of bad publicity, the company hired Lynn Martin, former labor secretary and Illinois congresswoman and present Deloitte & Touche consultant, to investigate Mitsubishi's sexual harassment policies and practices and to make recommendations for change. (During her tenure at the Labor Department, a glass ceiling commission had been established to investigate why more women weren't entering the ranks of upper management.) She submitted her "Model Workplace Plan for Mitsubishi" on February 12, 1997, recommending thirty-four steps to move the company toward becoming a model workplace, including the establishment of a "Zero Tolerance Task Force" and the revamping of the company's sex-

---

41. "Sexual Harassment Case against Mitsubishi Motor Manufacturing of America: Key Developments Timeline, December 1994–June 1998," *Pantagraph* (Bloomington-Normal, Ill.), http://www.pantagraph.com/mmmtime.html.

42. Ireland and Jackson only rescinded their boycott in January 1997, when they were convinced that the company was sincere in its efforts to repair their working environment.

43. "Mitsubishi Settlement Talk Isn't Backed with Action; EEOC Says No Attempt at Deal Has Been Made," *Chicago Tribune*, April 26, 1996.

ual harassment procedures.[44] Her selection, however, did little to alter Mitsubishi's downward spiral of bad press.

On April 28, 1997, days after Martin met with Mitsubishi Motor Company's Japanese board of directors, MMMA announced that it would replace the top officer of the company, chairman Tsuneo Ohinouye, and that he would retire in June but still serve as a consultant to the company. A source at the company claimed that the change was made because some officials were resisting Martin's recommendations, but a plant spokesman denied that interpretation.[45] In contrast to Astra USA's quick suspension of its chief executive, MMMA dragged its feet for a year after the EEOC had filed its case, incalculably damaging the company's reputation.

By March 1998 Mitsubishi must have realized that its legal predicament was fairly hopeless. The Seventh Circuit Court of Appeals spurned the company's attempt to overturn the district court's ruling that the case could go to trial as a "pattern or practice" case (in effect, a class action case). Faced with a trial that the EEOC anticipated would begin in September, the company was running out of delaying tactics. On the public relations front, matters were also at an impasse. Lynn Martin's $2 million fee, the adoption of her recommendations for new sexual harassment policies and women-friendly practices, and the hiring of new personnel officials to implement the new practices had only created another embarrassing fiasco. Mitsubishi's new head of human resources resigned, stating that "he had been coached to

44. "Recommendations to Mitsubishi Motor Manufacturing of America to Achieve a Model Workplace," February 12, 1997, http://www.martintaskforce.com/release.htm.

45. "2 Mitsubishi Execs Stepping Down: Anti-Harassment Project Continues," *Chicago Sun-Times*, April 30, 1997.

imply a degree of change within our organization . . . which did not exist."[46]

By April 1998 the company was ready to capitulate. After six years of intransigence, investigations, legal wrangling, and disastrous publicity, Mitsubishi, at the urging of district court judge Joe Billy McDade, and under the supervision of a special master appointed by the court, agreed to enter settlement talks with the EEOC. With the company facing trial and potential exposure of $90 million or more in compensatory and punitive damages,[47] its officers must have realized how costly and dangerous it would have been to go to trial with the massive amount of evidence against it that the EEOC had already managed to amass and with MMMA's sorry history of belligerence a matter of public record. At last, the broadest and potentially the costliest of the EEOC's sexual harassment suits was about to be resolved.

On June 11, 1998, both sides announced that they had reached a consensus and would sign and submit a consent decree for the court's approval. Judge Abner Mikva, the court-appointed special master, deemed it a "fair settlement designed to accelerate the creation of a workplace that is free of sexual harassment. . . . This is a win-win situation for the company, for the EEOC, and most of all, for the employees."[48] Kohei Ikuta, the executive vice president of Mitsubishi, admitted that the com-

46. The EEOC attained a copy of this letter of resignation through a discovery process in their lawsuit against the company. "Court Rules for Trial in Mitsubishi Sexual Harassment Suit," *Washington Post*, March 24, 1998.

47. The Civil Rights Act of 1991 placed caps on compensatory and punitive damages of $300,000 per individual plaintiff. With approximately three hundred aggrieved women claimed by the EEOC, and perhaps more in the class of female Mitsubishi workers that the EEOC claimed to represent, the potential liability of the company could have exceeded this $90 million figure.

48. "Mitsubishi Motor Manufacturing and EEOC Reach Voluntary Agreement to Settle Harassment Suit," EEOC press release, June 11, 1998.

pany did have a sexual harassment problem and that it had been trying for twenty months to implement better practices. "We acknowledge and respect the EEOC's authority to pursue equal employment opportunity and we look forward to working with the EEOC as a partner in progress," he stated. Mitsubishi agreed to pay $34 million in damages to the affected women, dwarfing the $9.5 million that Astra USA had paid in February, at that time the EEOC's largest settlement of a sexual harassment case. The Mitsubishi settlement did much to silence those liberal critics of the EEOC who had argued that it was ineffective.[49]

Among other nonmonetary relief, MMMA agreed to have its policies and complaint procedures monitored for three years by a panel of decree monitors, to allow a complaint monitor to hear appeals, to implement a "Zero-Tolerance Policy and Equality Objectives" that would prevent sexual harassment and forbid retaliation, to change its complaint procedures to encourage reporting of sexual harassment, to investigate all complaints within three weeks and take action within seven days, and to provide mandatory sexual harassment training programs for all employees. Mitsubishi's management and supervisors were also enjoined from engaging in sex discrimination, harassing or intimidating women, permitting a work environment hostile to women, and retaliating against any employee who opposed sexual harassment, filed charges, or received part of the monetary award.[50] Mitsubishi further agreed that the EEOC would have sole discretion in determining who would be eligible to receive

49. Other critics, from the right, had tried to prune the agency's budget during the Reagan and Bush era, and they, presumably, were not mollified ("presumably" because their reactions were not solicited in the press coverage that a Lexis/Nexis search uncovered).

50. "Joint Motion for Entry of Consent Decree," submitted to the U.S. District Court for the Central District of Illinois (Peoria Division), June 11, 1998, p. 4. The UAW local that represented Mitsubishi workers also joined the Consent Decree.

the $34 million settlement and how much each woman would receive (subject to court approval), with $300,000 the maximum amount that any one person could be awarded.[51]

What is astounding about this case is how persistently dense Mitsubishi's top management and counsel remained through their six-year ordeal. How, with all the publicity that sexual harassment cases had received—from the Anita Hill/Clarence Thomas hearings to the navy Tailhook incident to the peccadillos of Senator Robert Packwood (R., Oregon)[52]—could MMMA have devised such an ill-starred public relations debacle as the Chicago demonstration? Even more inexplicable is the legal strategy pursued by the company's inside and outside counsel, all of whom should have been aware of how neatly the EEOC's evidence against the company fit within the legal parameters of hostile environment sexual harassment (along with some incidents that would qualify as quid pro quo sexual harassment). With high-profile cases leading to large damage awards—as in the case of a secretary who accused a law partner at Baker and MacKenzie of fondling her breasts and received a $7.1 million award (later reduced to $3.5 million)[53]—how did this company expect to prevail when the EEOC claimed four hundred harassers, not just one? The EEOC knew that such a strong case would

51. That is the cap specified by the Civil Rights Act of 1991.

52. In June 1992, a female navy lieutenant went public with revelations of a "gauntlet" of groping officers who had assaulted women at the Tailhook Association's convention in Las Vegas in September 1991, and of the navy's lackluster investigation. The secretary of the navy and several admirals eventually lost their positions over failing to adequately investigate the charges, and the lieutenant was awarded $1.7 million in compensatory damages and $5 million in punitive damages from the hotel for lax security (reduced slightly on appeal) and $400,000 from the Tailhook Association. Senator Packwood was accused by several former female employees of groping them. Other charges of sexual harassment against prominent individuals would follow.

53. The amount exceeds the federal cap of $300,000 because various state charges were included.

send a message throughout the business community and encourage the filing of even more sexual harassment complaints with the commission.

Whether one is an admirer of federalizing sexual harassment under Title VII's ban on sex discrimination or not (and I am not),[54] it is impossible to deny that some very questionable behavior was tolerated and even encouraged at this Normal, Illinois, plant. Physical violence, threats of retaliation, and sexual assaults are all criminal matters. Gross sexual innuendos, sex parties encouraged by management and organized on company time, supervisors bullying probationary workers for sexual favors, and "frat boy" behavior by supervisors and employees are all clearly forbidden under the courts' interpretation of Title VII and ethically questionable by most people's standards. It is to these moral issues that we next turn.

The Moral Landscape

Normal, Illinois, is a typical mid-Western, largely blue-collar, agricultural city of ninety thousand, with the Mitsubishi plant, which rolled out its first automobiles in 1988, serving as its third-largest employer.[55] A particularly troubling aspect of the sexual harassment imbroglio at the plant is that when a company's management appears to turn a blind eye to behavior ranging from the criminal to the tortious to the indecent to the childishly ill-mannered, a subterranean hostility toward women appeared to be just waiting for an opportunity to emerge. Women have not been enthusiastically received by factory workers, who often

---

54. I have argued elsewhere for a new tort of sexual harassment, rather than federalization of the problem under Title VII. "Sexual Harassment as Sex Discrimination: A Defective Paradigm," *Yale Law & Policy Review* 8, no. 2 (1990).

55. "Women: The Motor Show," *The Guardian* (London), April 15, 1996.

view them as displacing men from increasingly scarce, high-paying, unionized manufacturing jobs. At Mitsubishi this animus extended through the ranks of management. Many of Mitsubishi's male workers—the EEOC claimed some four hundred—evinced a contempt for their female coworkers that, unchecked by management, ran riot. An ineffective sexual harassment policy and a management that seemingly overlooked or even condoned such practices encouraged the unseemly behavior to escalate. Leslie Wolfe, director of the Center for Women Policy Studies, pointed out that, at the time the EEOC filed suit, "if the corporate culture of your workplace validates the abuse, then mob mentality prevails."[56]

Despite complaints to the company, the union, and even local police dating back to 1990, charges filed with the EEOC by several women in 1992, a private lawsuit alleging sexual harassment and sex discrimination filed in 1994, and an EEOC investigation also dating from that year, the company did nothing to alter the pattern of abuse and mistreatment experienced by 300 (and the EEOC thought even more) of its female employees. Cultural differences may have played some part in upper management's obliviousness to harassment and, then, the truculence of the company in its relations with the EEOC, but it is difficult to assign complete fault to the company's 70 Japanese men, who comprised upper management. Middle management, the province of local American managers, allowed the "hostile environment" to simmer, and as John Hendrickson, EEOC's regional attorney, pointed out, "I've been doing sexual harassment litigation for years and I don't think any culture's got a lock on it."[57]

By 1990, when women first began to complain of sexual harassment at the plant, Mitsubishi's management and counsel

56. Ibid.
57. Ibid.

should have been well aware of the legal landscape of Title VII sex discrimination and of the potential liability that their company faced from such charges. The federal courts, as we saw earlier, had been reading sexual harassment into Title VII's ban on sex discrimination since the mid-1970s, and the Supreme Court solidified this trend in its first sexual harassment decision in 1986. As public attention became fixated on the issue in 1991, with the Clarence Thomas hearings and other high-profile incidents that followed, MMMA's Japanese upper management, its general counsel and its middle managers should have been well aware of the company's legal obligations. Consultants plied the land, warning companies of their legal jeopardy, hawking their wares, offering training manuals, videos, and management-coaching sessions. Foreign-owned subsidiaries doing business in the United States, as pointed out earlier, are subject to U.S. equal employment laws,[58] which should have been well known to the company.

In short, it is difficult to comprehend Mitsubishi's management's utter indifference to its legal peril to the bitter end. Its *imprudence* was almost boundless. *Prudence* is a part of most moral systems, usually not the highest moral virtue, the *summum bonum*, but an instrumental good, that is, a good that helps a person achieve the higher (or highest) moral virtue. Alternatively, prudence is considered to be a good in itself, a good of practical life. Prudence is ordinarily understood as handling one's own affairs well, carefully managing one's life, acting with due diligence or deliberation.

For a company doing business abroad, it is clearly a counsel of *prudence* to understand the legal landscape in which one is operating, or to engage attorneys who do, and to operate one's

58. With the minor exception for conflicting treaty obligations, an exception that did not apply in Mitsubishi's situation (see note 19).

business in a manner that conforms with the laws of the country in which one is operating. To do otherwise is to put one's business in jeopardy, to neglect one's stockholders' interests, and to imperil the bottom line. Mitsubishi's management was remiss on all these counts. It failed to put itself in the best legal position by not adopting sexual harassment guidelines and complaint procedures that the EEOC had been advocating for years and that most corporations had adopted. It neglected stockholder interests by exposing the company to a deluge of scathing media notoriety and legal liability. It worsened the bottom line of a company already in the red by incurring some $44 million in damages and large legal costs. Mitsubishi dealerships, and other product lines bearing the Mitsubishi name, although technically separate corporations, were also plagued by the bad publicity garnered by their recalcitrant associates.[59]

Corporations wishing to conduct business abroad may confront three sorts of environments that raise moral issues. (1) In some countries, a foreign law may just look *different* from what one is accustomed to and perhaps *less than ideal*. (2) In other nations, a particular law or practice may seem *clearly morally defective*, without being so egregious that it puts the legitimacy of the entire system into moral jeopardy. (3) In others, the economic or political system or both may be so debased that doing business there would raise a *grave moral challenge*.

Examples of the third category, the most serious, include paying off mobsters in Moscow, Russia, so that one's employees do not end up blown to bits on the way to the office; bribing government officials at every turn in the normal course of business; slipping large sums of money to Third World politicians so

59. Mitsubishi is part of one of the largest Japanese conglomerates, made up of about 150 separate but loosely aligned businesses with, in some cases, interlocking directorates.

that they do not nationalize one's business; standing by as these kleptocrats use that extorted money to finance a tribal war of subjugation; trading in goods produced by political prisoners in China; or doing business in totalitarian states that deprive their people of life, liberty, and property, like Nazi Germany or the old Soviet Union. All these scenarios pose a *grave moral challenge* for businesspeople abroad, and they are well beyond the scope of *prudence.*

At the opposite extreme is category one: laws that are just *different* or *less than ideal,* such as different corporate law; different tax law; different employment law. These laws do not raise any moral qualms at all but rather involve educating oneself about a different legal milieu. In this category, prudence recommends that the foreign business should operate in conformity with local law.

In between the two extremes is our second category of particular laws that seem *clearly morally defective* but are not so pervasive that they condemn the entire system. Here, one may confront a tax regime that is confiscatory or a law that requires business to exclude certain groups from employment or contract and property laws that are so underdeveloped or erratically enforced that the fruits of one's labor are insecure.

Although bright lines are difficult to draw between these three categories, and people will draw them differently, the categories do provide some rough-and-ready guidance. Where *grave moral challenges* (category three) are posed by endemic bribery, prison labor, or deprivation of freedom, a businessperson ought to seriously consider not engaging in business in that country because the country's entire system is abhorrent or rights-violating (depending on one's preferred moral terminology). If the problem is less systemic, falling into the second category (*clearly morally defective*), then one might try to change the bad laws or protest them or threaten to take one's business elsewhere until the problem is remedied. The first and least morally challenging category (*different* or *less than ideal*) requires that businesspeople exercise prudence and comply with the law.

Clearly, Mitsubishi was not operating in a category three situation. The U.S. political and economic system is not gravely defective. Doing business in the United States did not pose a grave moral challenge. Nor, I think, did it face a category two predicament of a law (the courts' interpretation of Title VII as prohibiting sexual harassment) that was so *clearly morally defective*, necessitating resistance or compelling a need to change the law through the legal process or by threatening to take one's business elsewhere.[60] If Mitsubishi thought that it faced a category two situation—and reasonable people might differ—it should have *never* raised a moral objection to the law or declared that it thought sexual harassment was a moral right or morally good or that it was the victim of a bad law. It never did any of this. Rather, company spokesmen paid lip service to the law,

---

60. As I have written elsewhere (see note 54), I do not think that a federal remedy is the best way of handling those instances of sexual harassment that violate the rights of victims. I would prefer a tort remedy, to be heard as other torts are by state courts. Also, I think that the courts have been overbroad in their interpretation of what constitutes sexual harassment, getting dangerously close to restricting the personal freedom and free speech rights of those among us who delight in telling the dirty joke, displaying the offensive pinup, or acting in suggestive, boorish ways that we used to just consider in bad taste. I do not welcome a federal agency snooping around the workplace, taking a few complaints as an invitation to wage an extensive, free-wheeling investigation of a company's employment practices. But that is the law, that is partly how Title VII was written and partly how it has been expanded through judicial interpretation. Given how outrageous some of the behavior was at Mitsubishi, whether one approves of all or most aspects of our present sexual harassment legal regime, Mitsubishi's employees stepped over anybody's line. Threats, acts of violence, assaults, outrageous acts designed to inflict emotional duress, threats by supervisors to fire new hires who did not comply with their sexual overtures: all of this is beyond the pale, and should not be the workplace experience of anyone, female or male.

declaring their adherence to equal opportunity laws, and their disapproval of sexual harassment, but denying that harassment had occurred on their watch. When the EEOC filed suit, the general counsel did tell employees that he thought that the EEOC was on a political quest to redeem itself at the company's expense and that the company was fighting big government, but this did not play well in the media and was not meant as a serious challenge to the morality of the law. Such statements might have been more persuasive had they been made by a company with a clearer conscience.[61] Thus, Mitsubishi's situation fell within category one (merely *different* laws), and the company should have made its policies and practices conform to the law. The company merely had to exercise prudence, but it failed miserably.

Prudence would counsel that managers doing business in another country sensitize themselves to the differing cultural values and popular sentiments that may affect their businesses. Mitsubishi's management failed miserably on this score as well. Although Japan did ban sex discrimination in employment in the late 1980s, that prohibition is rarely enforced, and the penalties are nugatory on the few occasions when it is. Only twenty sexual harassment suits have been filed in Japan, and the awards or settlements have been in the $10,000 range.[62] Japanese culture, especially its business culture, is still much more traditional than America's in respect to the roles of the two sexes. Women are

61. Indeed, my first reaction to hearing of Mitsubishi's demonstration against the EEOC was—great, finally a company is standing up to the EEOC. However, it is difficult to read the EEOC's case against Mitsubishi, and the statements by so many different women attesting to similar experiences, without realizing that the company was not defending principle, but merely attempting to cover up its own dismal practices.

62. "Japanese Women Challenge Sexual Harassment," *Feminist News*, May 1996, reporting on an article from the *Washington Post*, May 1, 1996.

expected to be "office ladies," if they work at all, and to quit the workaday realm once they marry. As married women, they are expected to tolerate their husbands' late-hour socializing at bars with their coworkers, drinking, and flirting with hostesses. The sex parties held by Mitsubishi management and staff, and attended by visiting Japanese executives, and the training sessions for Americans in Japan that culminated in visits to sex bars, probably would not raise many eyebrows in Japan.

Although traditional sex roles are changing—as Western mores continue to influence Japanese culture and as more women enter the workplace with the expectation of a lifetime of employment—customary relations have been much slower to change in Japan than in the United States and Western Europe. This may partly explain why Astra USA's parent company took a more active role in containing its subsidiary's sexual harassment scandal than did Mitsubishi's: Swedish management expressed its wish to comply with investigators and sent Swedish managers to the United States to investigate and cooperate with American authorities; Japanese management issued a pale statement about complying with American sexual discrimination law and a wish to settle the matter but took no further action. Astra's parent company acted prudently; Mitsubishi's did not.

Undeniably, Mitsubishi's Japanese executives failed miserably on this aspect of prudence in respecting cultural mores when doing business abroad. They unerringly did the wrong thing at every stage of the long, drawn-out battle. The demonstration in Chicago was the most conspicuous but by no means the only example of their imprudence.

Legal obligations and moral obligations are not coextensive. We can examine our legal obligations from a moral perspective to see whether law conforms to morality and, thus, whether we are dealing with good (or at least, acceptable) laws. Having considered the moral ramifications of Mitsubishi's legal position, we can conclude that *prudence* alone should have kept the company on a less catastrophic course. Although the company was not in a legal situation that raised higher-order moral concerns (i.e., category one or three), morality may require more than the law does, even when the law is good. For example, the law may direct us not to kill, but it might be silent on whether we are obliged to save someone else's drowning child.

Leaving the law aside, let us see what morality might have directed Mitsubishi's management to do about the sexually hostile working environment in its plant. Contemporary business ethics is represented by four major moral perspectives,[63] yet it is difficult to see how any of these systems would exonerate Mitsubishi's course. *Utilitarians* follow a "consequentialist"[64] approach to morality, counseling that happiness is the greatest good that a person can attain and pain the worst condition and one to be sedulously avoided. Their favored maxim for social action is to act in a way that maximizes the happiness of society and minimizes the pain. A refined version of utilitarianism favored by contemporary utilitarians is "rule utilitarianism," which urges moral actors to follow general rules designed to maximize social utility.[65] A utilitarian would be hard pressed to

63. For a utilitarian approach see William C. Starr, "Codes of Ethics—Towards a Rule-Utilitarian Justification," *Journal of Business Ethics* 2 (1983): 99–106. For a Kantian approach see: Jacquie L'Etang, "A Kantian Approach to Codes of Ethics," *Journal of Business Ethics* 11 (1996): 737–44. And for virtue ethics see: Steven M. Mintz, "Aristotelian Virtue and Business Ethics Education," *Journal of Business Ethics* 15 (1996): 827–38; and Janes E. Macdonald and Caryn L. Beck-Dudley, "Are Deontology and Teleology Mutually Exclusive?" *Journal of Business Ethics* 13 (1994): 615–23.

64. "Consequentialists" look to the effects of actions, assessing their moral worth by the consequences that result from selecting a particular course of action, rather than from the motivation of the actor.

65. "Rule utilitarianism" was a reaction to criticisms leveled against utilitarianism in its original, "act utilitarian" version since this version was subject to obvious problems, as in the following example: a utilitarian would have to

see how condoning acts of verbal abuse, physical threats, quid pro quo sexual propositions by supervisors, lewd and derisive remarks, and exposing oneself to coworkers could be seen as maximizing social happiness. When the pain of the women is balanced against the happiness experienced by the male perpetrators, the social utility has to be negative. It's difficult to see how any rule could be drafted that would lead to the maximization of social welfare based on deprecating others.

Similarly, for *Kantians*, those who prefer Immanuel Kant's "deontological"[66] moral perspective, it is hard to see how sexual harassment and management's failure to stop it can be morally justified. For Kantians, moral actors are urged to look at the nature of an act, rather than its consequences, and to never use other people simply for one's own purposes but always to treat them as ends in themselves. What this means/ends language evokes, and why it is popular among philosophers today, is that the human dignity of each person should be honored by every other person and that the interests of others should be taken into account in our moral calculations. Kant's "categorical imperative," his moral maxim, is a variant of the golden rule: Always treat other people so that the principle upon which one acts could be made a universal rule. If one wishes to steal from one's neighbor, that rule, if universalized, would lead to social depre-

---

endorse the killing of one innocent person to save the lives of five other people because that would maximize society's happiness.

66. "Deontological" moral systems look at the motivation—the good heart, one might say—of the actor, rather than the consequences that the act may have in the real world. For example, one may choose not to warn a neighborhood that a sexual predator is being released from jail. One may have acted out of respect for the freedom and dignity of the rapist, feeling that a person who has served his time should not have further penalties of ostracism heaped on him. If the rapist then goes on to rape and kill another victim, then one's action in not warning has had bad consequences, even though by failing to warn, one acted out of a good heart.

dation. With everyone stealing from everyone else, social chaos would result. Do not covet thy neighbor's property, in contrast, if made a universal rule, would lead to an exchange economy, heightened productivity, and social harmony. A Kantian would find no merit in a rule universalizing the kinds of sexual predation practiced on the line at Mitsubishi. Harassers clearly used women as a "means" for their own amusement or to express feelings of hostility toward the opposite sex, not as "ends" having equal moral dignity. Mitsubishi's failure to hold its factory workers and supervisors to a universalizable maxim clearly violates Kant's categorical imperative: One cannot universalize such a maxim as everyone should expose himself or herself to everyone else, call each other "bitch" and "cunt" (or their male equivalents), or hold the jobs of subordinates hostage to the sexual gratification of supervisors.

Another moral perspective that has influenced recent discussions in business ethics is "virtue theory" (or "virtue ethics"), which looks at the roles people play within corporations and how they ought to act, eschewing larger questions of politics and which moral system, utilitarian or Kantian, ought to be favored. Virtue theorists prefer to examine particular ethical dilemmas that face people in business, rather than trying to formulate preconceived general rules. It is an inductive method of case-by-case "muddling our way through," which owes much to Aristotle's approach to ethics of refining our judgments in real life situations. Individual virtue and integrity are what matters on this account of morality.[67] If individuals in business display integrity, then good corporate behavior and social responsibility will be the result. From this moral perspective, it is difficult to see how

67. This definition is taken from Stephen Maguire, "Business Ethics: A Compromise Between Politics and Virtue," *Journal of Business Ethics* 16, nos. 12–13 (September 1997): 1411–13.

high officials of Mitsubishi acted virtuously by ignoring or seeming to condone sexual harassment. A virtuous manager, presumably, would have taken the initial complaints of the women seriously, would have investigated in good faith, and would have taken disciplinary actions against offenders. The corporate culture that evolved by ignoring the early incidents, or just making offenders watch a thirty-minute video, encouraged, rather than minimized, disrespect for women. Managers later compounded the problems by stonewalling the EEOC and none too secretively organizing and funding a demonstration against it. Virtue theory would condemn practically every move that Mitsubishi made, from promulgating an ineffective sexual harassment policy and procedures that discouraged complaints to failing to remedy its problems with sexual harassment over a four-year period to its bizarre reaction to the EEOC's lawsuit.

One additional moral theory, "natural rights/natural law," would also lead to a condemnation of Mitsubishi's corporate culture of rampant sexual harassment and its hostile environment toward women. Natural rights theory holds that each person has inherent rights to life, liberty, and property that other people must respect; natural law maintains that there are universal laws of morality and law that ought to be observed, despite cultural differences, time, and place. A natural rights/natural law theorist might be skeptical about forcing a company to hire women, or any other "protected group," under Title VII. In fact, such a theorist would be critical of any piece of legislation such as Title VII that tells employers whom they must hire and what criteria they must not employ in making hiring decisions: race, religion, sex, national origin, color (and by later legislation, pregnancy, handicap, age, and immigration status).

Given this libertarian abhorrence of governmental interference with freedom of contract and distaste for EEOC-type wide-ranging investigations of a company's operations (which libertarians see as big government meddling), what would a natural rights perspective counsel once Mitsubishi had employed women as well as their much-preferred men? An essential component of a right to liberty is to be free from force or threats of force. Many women working in the plant were subjected to these sorts of rights violations on a fairly regular basis. Mitsubishi's management failed to prevent recurrences, and some of these acts amounted to criminal actions: threats, intimidation, sexual assaults, defacement of personal property. Other offensive behavior was obnoxious, irritating, defamatory, and so on. A natural rights theorist would distinguish between jokes to which a woman takes offense and sexual battery, but, in general, the natural rights perspective would lead to roughly the same conclusion as the other moral positions: that Mitsubishi's male employees and management acted with scant regard for the welfare of women and with a misguided toleration for rights violations against women.

Even if there were no laws against sexual harassment, a natural rights perspective would demand that management put a stop to those serious incidents of sexual harassment that led to rights violations. On the milder forms of what some people still consider sexual harassment, a natural rights theorist might differ from the other three moral perspectives. As for the off-color jokes, the sharing of sleazy pictures, and attendance at sex parties, a company would be well within its property rights to restrict employees from engaging in such activity *on the company's property*. Workers who wanted to engage in such activities could look elsewhere for employment.[68] In contrast, on natural rights

68. Some libertarians might argue that the women are the ones who should quit and look elsewhere for employment if they do not wish to live with the constant sexual bantering and worse that epitomized Mitsubishi's corporate culture. I would agree with that, were it not for the seriousness of some of the harassment, which amounted to criminal or tortious behavior. A corporate cul-

principles, a company like Hooters would be well within its property rights to build a business that tolerates these lesser forms of "sexual harassment" of waitresses by customers, as long as the waitresses voluntarily agree to subject themselves to such treatment. (Indeed, Hooters' waitresses signed such an agreement as a condition of employment.)

In many issues of business ethics, these four moral systems lead to conflicting recommendations, to dilemmas, and, at the least, to differences in emphasis. Here, however, the different theories display remarkable agreement in condemning the most serious sexually hostile acts displayed by Mitsubishi's male employees toward women and the indifference of the company's management to remedying the situation.

Conclusion

Mitsubishi's management failed to act prudently by displaying an indifference to American law and social sensibilities. As a result, it paid a heavy price in legal damages and an even more significant price in bad publicity that adversely affected an already weak corporate balance sheet. Japanese culture may have played a part in management's ineptness, but many other Japanese companies, including automobile manufacturers, operate in the United States without notoriety of this sort. Prudence, alone, without other higher moral scruples against the mistreatment of women, should have prevented the company from resisting the EEOC to the point that it filed a massive lawsuit and even two years beyond. Indeed, prudence alone should have caused the company to reexamine its sexual harassment policies and com-

---

ture of old-boy dirty joking would be another story, entirely. If you don't like the jokes, then resign and go elsewhere.

plaint procedures when the first complaints were filed with the EEOC in 1992, if not in 1990, when the earliest internal complaints arose. At no stage in the eight-year ordeal did the company exercise prudence. Finally, after it had lost so many court battles that a trial could no longer be staved off, management acceded to court-mediated settlement discussions.

Diverse moral philosophies are as one in condemning Mitsubishi's corporate acquiescence and indifference to the mistreatment of many women by their coworkers and supervisors. It is unseemly, and morally blameworthy, for people in positions of corporate power to extort sexual favors, to make putting up with threats and intimidation of all sorts a condition of employment or to look the other way and allow such practices to continue, and to seem to approve of such behavior by taking no action or ineffective action. Even if such behavior had not been prohibited by law, moral businesspeople should not have tolerated it.

Mitsubishi's public relations debacle is a good case study of how a corporation should not act when it is doing business in a morally acceptable foreign land (that is, a category one or, perhaps, two). Knowledge of the law of the land, sensibility to the culture of the country in which one is doing business—simple prudence—should go a long way toward avoiding such self-inflicted wounds.

Index